# LONG TIME COMING

# LONG TIME COMING

## RECKONING WITH RACE IN AMERICA

## MICHAEL ERIC DYSON

**THORNDIKE PRESS**
A part of Gale, a Cengage Company

Copyright © 2020 by Michael Eric Dyson.
Thorndike Press, a part of Gale, a Cengage Company.

**ALL RIGHTS RESERVED**
Thorndike Press® Large Print Black Voices.
The text of this Large Print edition is unabridged.
Other aspects of the book may vary from the original edition.
Set in 16 pt. Plantin.

**LIBRARY OF CONGRESS CIP DATA ON FILE.
CATALOGUING IN PUBLICATION FOR THIS BOOK
IS AVAILABLE FROM THE LIBRARY OF CONGRESS.**

ISBN-13: 978-1-4328-8706-3 (hardcover alk. paper)

Published in 2021 by arrangement with St. Martin's Publishing

Printed in Mexico
Print Number: 01    Print Year: 2021

To
**LeBron James**
Greatest basketball player on the globe
In the conversation for G.O.A.T.
Founder of the *I Promise School* for at-risk
  children
Media mogul
Global business magnate
Transformative philanthropist
Outspoken social activist who refused to
  shut up and dribble
Started at the bottom, now you're here
For standing with Black people without
  excuse or apology
And for embracing people of all races
  around the world

"Black men, Black women, Black kids, we
are terrified. . . . You have no idea how that
cop that day left the house. . . . You don't
know if he had an argument at home with
his significant other. You don't know if his
kids said something crazy to him and he left
the house steaming. Or maybe he just left
the house thinking that today is going to be
the end for one of these Black people. That's
what it feels like. It hurts."

— LeBron James

It's been a long, a long time coming
But I know a change gon' come,
oh yes it will
— Sam Cooke,
"A Change Is Gonna Come"


For the Lord of hosts will have a day
of reckoning
Against everyone who is proud
and lofty
And against everyone who is lifted up,
That he may be abased.
— Isaiah 2:12

# CONTENTS

# CONTENTS

When my sons were in high school and pictures of Philando Castile were on the front page of the *Times,* I wanted to burn all the newspapers so they would not see the gun coming in the window, the blood on Castile's T-shirt, the terror in his partner's face, and the eyes of his witnessing baby girl. But I was too late, too late generationally, because they were not looking at the newspaper; they were looking at their phones, where the image was a house of mirrors straight to Hell.

— ELIZABETH ALEXANDER

# PRELUDE:
## GOLD ORB

Dear Elijah McClain,

I write to you out of profound grief. It is not easy to watch the Black bodies pile up in the streets and in our imaginations as we reckon with a racial catastrophe that has haunted this nation from its first breath. When I saw the video of your fatal encounter with the police, it literally made me — a grown Black man from the tough streets of Detroit teeming with mayhem and murders — weep almost uncontrollably. I suppose it was your sweet demeanor. I suppose it was your palpable innocence. I suppose it was the fact that a video was even posted. It told me from the start that the outcome wasn't going to be good, that you wouldn't survive, that your death would be another death that would happen as if it hadn't happened at all.

God, I thought, I fairly prayed, even begged, not this sweet young man, not this beautiful soul, not this humble spirit, not him, he cannot have posed a threat to anybody and surely not to cops armed with guns and batons and Tasers. All he had was a coat and a mask and a gentle bearing that enveloped his vulnerable soul as he was trying to get by on his own terms.

But those terms were soon to come to a cataclysmic end. The history of race would yet again be condensed into an interaction between the cops and a young Black anybody from Black anywhere doing Black anything on any given Black night. Yes, it was random, you were to that degree random, but it was a randomness that exists within a universe of perverse predictability that means any Black person can be targeted anywhere at any time. This reinforces the vulnerability that all of us Black folk share, and that you, sweet young Elijah, bore in your body on that fateful night.

Like all the Black deaths this nation has recently reckoned with, your loss was an egregious offense to humanity. You could have been our baby brother or son or grandson, anyone young whose life had just begun, who, like any soul, deserves to exist until time expires and space collapses in a natural rhythm of life and death. As is often the case for the Black dead, most of us got

14

to know your name only after you were gone. With the belated circulation of the video capturing the events that led to your death, we learned that you met your fate in Aurora, Colorado. We grieve for you still.

Just twenty-three, you were a tender-hearted, beautiful young man who, in your own words, was "different," because you did things like play the violin to soothe stray cats. Your co-worker said you seemed to walk with a gold orb around you. Someone called the cops on you, saying you appeared suspicious as you walked home from a convenience store in the summer of 2019, waving your arms. You wore a ski mask because your anemia made you get cold easily. When the cops arrived, you begged them to truly see you: "I am an introvert, please respect the boundaries that I am speaking." You told them you were on your way home and asked them to stop being so aggressive. The interaction quickly escalated as you, all of five feet six inches and 140 pounds, tried to speak to the cops, and they refused to listen; they applied a carotid hold to limit the blood flow to your brain, rendering you temporarily unconscious. And when the Aurora Fire Rescue arrived, they administered ketamine to you in an effort to sedate you, which, in combination with the trauma you endured, was enough to eventually kill you.

Elijah, your words that evening are heartbreaking. You tried so hard to convince the police that you were no threat to anyone and a good person, much the way that George Floyd tried to convince the cops that he was not a bad guy. The string of words that flowed from your mouth as the cops brutalized you is at once sad, because you tried your best to show that you were a meek and mild soul, and enraging, because it didn't matter what you said. They were hell-bent on smashing your body into no-thing-ness, into not-there-ness.

Elijah, you showed you were a sensitive and lovely soul. You did this despite enduring bouts of crying and vomiting. Elijah, you too, like Eric Garner and George Floyd, said, "I can't breathe." You told them, "I'm just different. That's all. I'm so sorry." You told them, "I have no gun. I don't do that stuff." You promised, "I don't do any fighting." Then you pleaded, "Why are you attacking me? I don't even kill flies. I don't eat meat!" — as if your penchant for peacefulness and your dietary discipline might somehow convince them that your life was worth sparing. But, Elijah, you quickly insisted that you didn't have a sense of moral superiority over those who disagreed with your choice: "But I don't judge people who do eat meat." You begged them to forgive you.

No, my lovely young friend, it is they who need to beg your forgiveness and be held accountable. Yes, it is true that a few months later one of the cops involved in your death, along with a couple of fellow officers, were fired because they took selfies near the site where you were killed, including one of the cops mimicking the very chokehold that led to your death, and as they did so they laughed with a cruelty that's hard to fathom. But that is not justice for you, Elijah. Those men who wantonly destroyed your body must be arrested and put on trial.

Dear, dear, sweet Elijah, we have said as a nation that we are now ready to handle our business and finally address systemic racism. The reckoning that is upon us has come about because of the tragic death of George Floyd, killed by a cop who kept his knee on Floyd's neck for more than nine minutes even as he cried out that he couldn't breathe. There was something vilely disorienting about the barbarism of the cop's action, as cool and casual an act of murder as many Americans had ever witnessed.

George Floyd was hardly the first Black

person to be killed by the cops, as you know all too well. But his death struck a nerve and forced us to confront the habits and systems that harm all of us. Though their experience is hardly equal, even white folk cannot truly enjoy the benefits of race, or the democracy on which they are supposed to rest, unless all of us, ultimately, are free.

Dear Elijah, permit me here to address those white folk for a bit.

My fellow Americans, I beg of you, first consider this: Do you realize how much faith it takes for me and those like me to write "my fellow Americans?" Do you realize how much energy it takes to summon the will to say those words? Do you realize how weary I am, how weary we are, millions of Black folk in this country — and right from the start it's a troubled we, a complicated we, a disputed we — of being denied recognition as Americans or even as human beings? Do you know that so many Black folk are still full of love for the nation that so often treats us so poorly? We are used to hearing presidents say "my fellow Americans," a phrase composed of a pronoun, adjective, and noun, to suggest the bond we share as citizens. Grammar is one thing, citizenship an entirely different affair. Has the sentiment ever really been true for

Black folk? Do we really live in the same country as white folk? Do we see the same things? Do we experience the same realities? Is our nation's motto fully realized: *E pluribus unum, "Out of many, one"*?

Dear Elijah, we are about to see if it is true that we are one, to see if your death and those of Ahmaud Arbery, George Floyd, Breonna Taylor, Hadiya Pendleton, Sandra Bland, Clementa Pinckney, and untold others are viewed as worthy of the moral revulsion and, from there, the change of practice and belief that would prove a real reckoning is taking place. Black death has hounded us from 1619 to this day. The theft of our bodies and futures, and our culture too, has offered the country unimaginable wealth, stability, and enjoyment. The blue plague has descended on our communities, the police bringing us terror from the plantation to the pavement. The wiles of white supremacy have seduced us, teaching us to hate and despise each other, and to take a cheap discount on justice, in ways that dishonor our best traditions. Black bodies have been killed and progress has been stalled to provide white comfort. But still, despite everything, we have continued, must continue, to hope.

Dear Elijah, the reckoning is upon us. It

may have come about suddenly, dramatically, this promising revolution, but it has been building up for centuries. It has been a long time coming. But it's up to us; it will only happen if we make it happen. Dear Elijah, do I believe that we have sufficient will and hope to make it real?

In the end, I reckon so.

Not a house in the country ain't packed to its rafters with some dead Negro's grief.
— BABY SUGGS, IN TONI MORRISON'S
*BELOVED*

# 1. BLACK DEATH

My dear Emmett Till,

The mere mention of your name whisks us to another time and place stained by the blood of martyrs and dripping with the hate of Black bodies. Of all the tragedies of your story — that you were a fourteen-year-old boy from up north who didn't know the byzantine bigotry of Mississippi, that your stuttering could sometimes be resolved by whistling, that you were kidnapped and killed in such a profane manner — perhaps the saddest is that you never got the chance to do what normal kids do. In a frightening flash you went from Chicago teenager to global icon of the civil rights movement. As important as you have been to my freedom, to our freedom, it would be better to have a world where it didn't make sense for a beautiful boy like you to have to die. It would be better to live in a country where you could have gone to church, scarfed down hot dogs, flirted with girls, hung out with your friends, talked trash on the basketball court, gotten married and had children, and taken your kids to visit your childhood home while doing what so many of us have done as well: apologize to our mothers for giving them the blues when we were hardheaded kids.

I think of you, a boy I never met, far more often than I should, far more than any of us who never met you should. Not because we shouldn't care about the fate of a boy we never met, but because the death of a boy we never met has taken on such outsize meaning. It reminds us always that boys like you, boys like we were, boys who are now ours, too, are just as vulnerable sixty-five years later. It is beyond absurd that the slightest perceived offense in the white mind should have such fatal consequences then or now. When I see carefree teens happy just to hang out with their friends and eat ice cream and play video games, I wonder what you might have done as you came of age in Chicago. I have seen the spark when teens get an inkling of what they might do for the rest of their lives, and it makes me sad to think you never had that joy.

I appeared on *Oprah* once with Myrlie Evers-Williams, Medgar Evers's widow and a leader in her own right, and your precious mother, Mamie Till-Mobley. I remember that Myrlie still pulsed with visceral rage at the snuffing out of Medgar, and that your mother's grief was as deep and palpable as it had been the day you perished. Mississippi murders melded the hearts of these women in an architecture of suffering and made of their spirits a living sepulcher for the man and boy they loved. Their breathing was a memorial, a fierce reminder that their loss was not theirs alone, but the loss of a nation.

Seeing them sit side by side, I couldn't help but reflect on how the third woman onstage, Oprah Winfrey, tied to Mississippi by birth, got to change the world, not by dying but by living, though she knew that her living owed a debt to you and Medgar. By having your mother and Myrlie on that set she got to pay homage to her roots and to offer you another platform to speak thirty-five years after we never heard from you again. I often wonder how your voice sounded, what others heard as you played at school or gave book reports in class, or what your voice would have sounded like as you matured and spoke up in Bible study or testified at prayer meetings in church. You have spoken to the ages, and yet we have been denied your voice.

It is weird to know you without ever getting to know you, to know you as a saint of sorts while not truly knowing the depth of a courage so stubborn that even your killers testified to it. I can only imagine the flush of fearlessness in a face so young even as mortal peril loomed. You refused to believe that these soulless goons were driving you to your death. And then after they did their evil and washed their hands of the entire affair in a court built for kangaroos and malignant liars, they seemed to get away with murder. But what they couldn't imagine is that their determination to silence your voice actually amplified the sound of a young preacher in Montgomery, Alabama, who spoke of you often, arguing that even though your death was caused by "two cruel men, the ultimate responsibility for this and other tragic events must rest with the American people themselves."

I wish I could say that your death changed things forever. But here we are, my brave young soldier of light, caught in the madness of hate once again. Long before your death, and so many times since then, we have pledged to reckon with the racial calamity at the heart of our democracy. And too many times we have reneged on that promise and failed to embrace our best racial future.

As I write, the cities of our country are burning once again because of Black death. A vicious virus is stalking the globe, a disease that — sadly, predictably — has attacked Black flesh with tragic specificity. The pandemic has thrust us into the vortex of Black vulnerability. In America, the coronavirus has exposed ugly truths that are far from novel. They are in fact part of the barely acknowledged preexisting condition of racial oppression. The abysmal lack of access to healthcare for our poorest people means that Black and Brown folk suffer higher rates and harsher consequences of heart disease, diabetes, and asthma and are far more likely to be exposed to the virus in the work they do. Black and Brown folk, paradoxically enough, stock the front lines of healthcare, and that, along with ringing cash registers and delivering food, greatly increases their susceptibility to COVID-19. Beyond the mathematical averages that sum up their vulnerability, Black and Brown suffering is far greater and bleaker — they are more likely to die from the deadly virus.

But the death I am speaking of here, dear Emmett, comes at the hands of white vigilantes, and, for the umpteenth time, at the hands of murderous cops. When America watched the video recording of policeman Derek Chauvin callously resting his knee and the full weight of his body on Minneapolis motorist George Floyd's neck for more than nine minutes, suffocating him, we were reminded that we were facing a dual pandemic united by one desperate cry: I can't breathe. In Minnesota it was recorded, again, for the world to see. And for the first time, many of our white fellow citizens have seen it too.

Dear Emmett, I must speak directly to our white brothers and sisters: So many of you, my white friends, have said that you now see that what we have been saying all along is true. But take a moment to let what we have seen for centuries sink in. Please understand that there is a great deal more heartbreak and tumult that you haven't seen behind what you are now finally beginning to see. Sight requires imagination. Imagination makes what we see make sense. Consider these videos visual autopsies of the slow death of justice.

Can you imagine how we feel when we see the moving pictures of yet another one of our people slaughtered in the streets? We speak in our day of triggers, moments that crystallize trauma, flood time with memory, and wash us into emotional peril. Triggers may be small things that spark remembrance of bigger and older things, and before we know it, we are paralyzed by panic and filled with fear. Or they can be seismic events that jar loose our collective memory of injury inflicted and pain endured. In this case it is the bitterly suppressed realization that American prosperity was built on Black death. Some Africans died in self-defense when they were ambushed by brutal catchers looking for new flesh to enslave. Many others succumbed on the unforgiving voyage to the New World and were unceremoniously tossed overboard. Those who reached North America were often murdered in the ruthless haste to build the American economy.

Beyond the loss of our bodies, we faced metaphysical death, too, since the nation cruelly imagined the nonbeing of Black folk. Whiteness had inherent value. Black life was morally and culturally deficient. Once slavery was over, Black existence was primarily useful, yet again, to serve whiteness. Your white forebears imagined a geography of racial separation to secure the American social contract. The game was rigged, the fix was in, and whiteness was declared the winner. It wasn't enough to make this a human arrangement: God was brought in to establish a divine inspiration for white supremacy. The white world burned crosses on Black folk's lawns to remind them of their place in the social and theological order. The trespass by Black bodies into white lunch counters or interracial marriage was legally forbidden. Sympathetic whites, like some of your mothers or fathers who aided or loved Black folk, were shunned. Black transgressors were berated or worse — threatened, and often killed.

Dear Emmett, as you tragically learned, the manner of Black death — by lynching, or stabbing and castration, or both; or by shooting, or asphyxiation, or being set ablaze in a pyre to light up the night; or by being kidnapped and then beaten and dumped into the river — was as varied and as arbitrary as its motive: a smirk, a smile, a pantomimed smooch, a disrespectful look, backtalk, the hint of Black equality, or just catching a white person in a bad mood on the wrong day when the only cure for his ill-tempered itch was to scratch a Black body off the list of the living. It was as casual an act as swatting a fly or crushing a bug beneath his feet.

Our bodies carry memory — not just our own, but the memory of the group as well.

We feel the history in our bones as much as we witness it with our eyes. The convulsions of racial distress on-screen twist in the pits of our stomachs. The combustions in the streets explode deep inside our psyches. The blood of our brothers and sisters clots in our arteries. Their death is our death. Their suffering is our own. Their scream for help is our scream for help. Their cries for relief are literally spoken with our tongue, as we mouth their last words. We speak back to them as we watch them go down to death, as if our words, uttered posthumously, might somehow reverse time and put us there in solidarity with our not yet fallen brother or sister. We talk to ourselves or to whoever is with us as we view Black death made into spectacle and sport. We say how we hate that the world is invading their privacy as their lives draw to a close. We say how we hate that their dignity has been robbed from them along with their lives. We say how we hate that we are watching something that should never happen.

There are things that are hard to say but even more difficult not to see. We cannot deny a tragic paradox: because a Black person's killing was caught on camera, the justice that eluded them in life, when they weren't treated as a human being, could only come in death, when their murder could be redressed. That is no consolation to the dead person and only sad consolation to their loved ones. Yes, there is redemption in some Black death, especially when we insist that a death provide moral utility for the living. Such a calculation is unavoidably selfish, especially when, unlike, say, a Martin Luther King Jr., who deliberately courted death in the course of his moral purpose, someone is killed who did not intend to die to help their race. In such cases we must remember that justice, like funerals, is for the living. The dead, the mercilessly slaughtered, are denied first their bodies, their being; then they are denied control over the social consequences of their nonbeing; finally, they are denied the very changes that only their deaths make possible.

My dear Emmett, this is the nature of Black life: there is an unkind ubiquity to unjust death. Any of us at any time might be its victim. The assault on Black life recognizes no noncombatants, no civilians. In this way there is an odd juxtaposition in the democracy of unjust Black death: you, Emmett, an ordinary teenage boy, became famous in the fight for justice because you were murdered, and Martin Luther King was murdered because he was famous for fighting injustice. The use we make of both your memories is a sign of how the Black body works even in death. Martyrdom rests on a brute and lopsided exchange: a Black figure dies, and may end up saving us, precisely because we can do little if anything to save them. With some Black deaths the ordinary become extraordinary, the anonymous are made famous, and their funerals are attended by the mighty and low alike because they all share a bond of Blackness that exceeds their circumstances. They are us, ordinary Black folk living, breathing, running, existing. We curse their assailants, their cold, callous, indifferent, brutal, hateful killers. We gasp involuntarily when we see yet another Black body drained of life, bullet by bullet, breath by breath; we are sickened, and then shocked, and then maddened, and then saddened, and then enraged.

Witnessing their deaths makes us fearful that we, or someone we know or love, might be next. We are ashamed that we feel lucky that it wasn't us. We feel guilty yet grateful for our fortune. But we fight hard to keep that fate from befalling us, or our children, or any other Black person. We feel at times irrationally guilty for not being there to help them. Yet we realize that others who witnessed their deaths couldn't stop them from dying either. And, of course, their killers have little incentive to let them live since they get such dark acclaim for slaying another Black body. We feel helpless in the face of these deaths — not only to stop the killers, but helpless to stop the next person from dying, until we are made to feel that we can't stop anyone from dying at all. Death by natural causes becomes a luxury, a fantasy of escape from a culture addicted to our death as fetish, as titillation.

My dear Emmett, all of this and so much more came flashing back to us when we witnessed Ahmaud Arbery running for his life on a street in his hometown in Georgia where he had every right to be. Emmett, let me ask our white brothers and sisters some questions: Can't you see that the notion that he didn't belong there, that his Black body was out of place, and therefore out of options, and then finally out of luck, is just one of so many troubling things? It makes us feel the anatomy of our nothingness, our bodies squeezed into formlessness and invisibility beneath the pressure of a whiteness that wills our inexorable nonbeing. Can you imagine what we feel when we see this man being hunted like an animal? When we see him literally running for his life? That he was suspected of being a thug because he looked at an unfinished home shows how things that white folk take for granted get Black lives taken. It is just fine for white folk to take a peek. But Black curiosity is criminal.

When one of Ahmaud's killers places a 911 call about a Black male, the dispatcher asks the caller what he is doing. The answer is remarkable for its sublime ordinariness: he is running down the street. That's it. But that doesn't stop the caller from fabricating a looming menace. His voice seems to betray puzzlement as to why the white female dispatcher doesn't immediately understand, or at least acknowledge, the code in which he is speaking, a code indicating that a Black man, breathing, alive, running, is on the loose, and the threat has to be contained or eliminated right now. The macabre prospect of heaping suspicion on Ahmaud's lean and muscular chocolate frame for no other reason than that it existed is no less the stuff of horror for its indecent normalcy. Without cause Ahmaud is deemed worthy of pursuit by a murderous father-and-son tag team who fetch their guns and jump in a white truck to hunt him down. You see, Ahmaud had offended a law of white racist physics: a Black body and a white body cannot exist in the same space and time without white permission.

That permission is premised on a hidden dimension of the violent compact of white supremacy: Black bodies that violate the rules of play automatically revert back to the conventions of slavery and the protocol of the plantation. The owner can do whatever he wishes with his property. Black bodies in white space are subject to the denial of rights, the suspension of mobility, and, at the discretion of their "owner," the cessation of life. During slavery and Jim Crow this understanding was baked, or rather lynched, into Black consciousness until it became muscle reflex and mental habit. In our day the law moves to the realm of the explicit only when a Black body is killed. For this law to thrive it must remain implicit, learned only through innuendo and inference.

The rules of the white world are communicated through cultural habits and social norms that reinforce Black fear and carry a message that cannot be missed: white spaces are sacred and not to be invaded or tarnished. (This brings to mind an early scene in the film *Get Out* where we know something awful is about to happen. We know the hero is in danger even though he is "just" walking down a suburban street after dark. It is a horror movie about the Black ordinary and the ordinary Black.) The law must be masked, its conditions muted, its application completely arbitrary. The owner need not claim provenance of a particular body in advance of the violation. The contract begins at birth for all Black bodies. The white owner can recall at will the life of any Black person who violates white space. In the minds of the marauding father and son Ahmaud is fair game because he knows the rules about not poking his head into white spaces and invading white neighborhoods but fails to heed them.

As if two white men tracking Ahmaud isn't enough, a third man joins the pursuit. The treacherous father and son try to cut Ahmaud off with their truck, but he doubles back to pass them. The man in the third car, who claims he was only a witness, tries to block him, but Ahmaud eludes him as well. Still, he can only do so much as they hunt him like a runaway slave. The father climbs atop the bed of the truck with a .357 Magnum in hand. Ahmaud runs away from the "witness" and back toward the hateful father and son. The "witness" is recording the frightening four-minute pursuit. Ahmaud is largely seen from a foreboding distance.

My dear Emmett, you may know a bit about such situations, since you may have realized right before your murder that you were in serious trouble. But, I ask white folk, can you imagine what Ahmaud experienced as he ran, and ran, and ran? Can you get inside his body and mind for a moment? Feel his heartbeat thumping in his chest. Imagine his fear and the adrenaline fueling his desperate attempt at escape. Run with him. Feel his sinews stretching, his body's equilibrium adjusting to the profoundly unsettling pursuit, his DNA violently transferred as his bodily composition will soon spill all over his killer's shirt, his blood testifying in splatters to the violent character of his death. Imagine as he is running what is running through his mind. He can feel the effect of the reversion to the rule of slavery and the law of Jim Crow in his body and in the air.

Unlike you, dear Emmett, he is from the South and old enough to know that white men on an isolated stretch of street in a rural community have often hidden their secrets of death inside the smashed or bullet-ridden skulls of unsuspecting Black bodies. Unlike you, dear Emmett, he is old enough to know that white men full of hate can justify their murder of Black bodies by claiming they were afraid for their lives. He is old enough to know that the laws were created for white men to stand their ground and bury Black bodies beneath it. He is old enough to feel the history of Black flight from white resentment course through his body. He is old enough to recall stories he heard, stories he was told, all a jumble, a blinding blur, since his breathing is now faster and shallower, his lungs beginning to hurt, his legs getting heavier beneath him, his arms flailing against the air as he wishes he could swipe away time and space to escape his pursuers' demonic persistence.

He is old enough to know that this won't end well, not without a fight, but, as always, it is never a fair fight. It is always cowardly white men insisting on their superiority who fall back on their weapons, their ropes, or their trucks in pursuit of the Black body. The Black body that in the not-too-distant past white men yearned to swing from a tree. Imagine all the pent-up rage that resided in the hollowed-out minds of those bigots that day. Imagine Ahmaud being caught amid whispering trees and the secrets they shed as he tears by in desperate flight. His breaths are shorter and shorter as he gasps for air. His feet are tired, but he keeps running. He doesn't fold. No doubt they envy his ability to escape as they hunt him. They feel the thrill of the chase, hunting a Black man like they were hunting for that evening's dinner. They feast on his death in advance of its inevitable occurrence.

They know they are going to shoot him as surely as he knows they are going to kill him. He hopes he can outrun them, make a dash down some side street and escape, but the terrain underfoot isn't his friend. The 911 call was a ruse, a sad, sorry effort to set the frame, made sadder by the fact that it often works. Not long after the call, the shotgun sounds, the pellets penetrate Ahmaud's body, and then, quickly, with fatal repetition, two more shots ring out. We see all of this because the "witness" is recording a video with his phone. Right before his fatal injuries we see Ahmaud try to escape by running toward his "witness," but he is forced back toward the father and son. The father yells, presumably, for Ahmaud to stop, calling his son's name as his son takes his first shot at close range, which hits Ahmaud in the chest, injuring his right lung, ribs, and sternum. Still Ahmaud bravely fights the son off. Ahmaud lunges forward and wrestles with him while the father observes and the witness continues to record. When the son blasts more buckshot into Ahmaud (who at that point, like the son, is briefly off camera), we see smoke burst from the barrel of the gun. The father has dropped his cellphone by then. Ahmaud is bleeding and throws another punch. The son fires a final shot, striking Ahmaud in his upper left chest. The son walks away in defiant triumph, holding his gun, as the father gets off the truck clutching his weapon. He rolls Ahmaud over, supposedly to see if he has a weapon. Of course he doesn't. But in the father and son's twisted logic, Ahmaud's Blackness is a weapon for the possession of which he must die. The police arrived a few seconds after Ahmaud fell, as he lay bleeding out. The witness later claimed that in the short interval before the cop showed up the son pronounced a racist benediction over his quick work of Black death: "Fucking nigger." Of course the cop took the father's word for what had happened and let him and his son go. After all, being a cop offered him complete understanding of the rules of reversion under which he was reared.

41

My dear Emmett, the malevolent pursuit of Ahmaud reveals another bruising paradox in Black life: even as quarters of white America loathe Black bodies, there is at once a lust for Blackness — yes, to control it, but also to get inside it, to be near something grudgingly admired. To be sure, it is the sort of admiration one has for any animal that is threatening, as one marvels at its strength and cunning, its pluck and crafty ingenuity. Such prowess is cheered when it flashes on the athletic field. When it ranges beyond the arena, it is feared, even stalked, subdued, and, if necessary, killed. So much of white society rests on mastering the animal menace of Blackness. The myth of Blacks as dangerous showed up in slavery, and in the Confederacy, when white supremacy took to horseback. It showed up, too, in Reconstruction's Black Codes, aimed at restricting Black mobility, and in sharecropping, where the slave plantation was reborn. The idea showed up as well during Jim Crow when oppression flowed in segregated water fountains, hotels, bars, and swimming pools. When we resist such efforts, it seems to confirm white fears. Our effort to shake off white obstruction and move forward reinforces the belief that we are dangerous animals in need of policing by white society.

It is little wonder that Black folk in our day think that a white citizen's belligerent demand to know if we belong in a certain neighborhood, coffee shop, car, or school harkens back to a time and place where we were culturally if not legally bound to answer such questions. In many ways, dear Emmett, this harkens back to your day. The rise of "Karen" and "Becky" and "Patty" as types and tropes of racial surveillance among white women is instructive. A disturbing habit has arisen: ordinary white women, neither empowered by the courts nor sanctioned by social services, demand that Black folk give account of their actions, their presence, or their intentions. Such demands (often captured on a video recording) are made to kids selling lemonade on the street, folk barbecuing in the local park, or a student stealing a few moments of shut-eye in an Ivy League university lounge. These women seem to believe their white skin and social privilege, both of which they are largely oblivious to but dependent on, have deputized them to handcuff Black liberty and to arrest Black mobility. When they call the cops, they are essentially calling for backup to reinforce their positions and validate their concerns. Most of them are surely aware of how calling the cops can easily lead to havoc for Black folk.

The white woman who called the cops on a Black man in Central Park because he asked her to leash her dog, as the rules dictate, is a perfect example. The woman became irate when the man began filming her after she denied his request. Amy Cooper, the white woman, then told the Black man, Christian Cooper, that she was going to call the cops to report that a Black man was endangering her. "There's an African American man, he's recording me and threatening me and my dog," Amy said to the police. Of course, it wasn't true that he was threatening her. When the cops came they chalked the incident up to a verbal dispute, and no one was arrested. But the video went viral. The next day Amy was fired by her employer because they wanted nothing to do with her racist behavior. She apologized, and Christian accepted her apology, although he suggested her actions pointed to underlying racism in the nation.

The particulars of their encounter testify to the delicate racial ecology that is so easily upset. Christian, a Harvard graduate and an avid birdwatcher, turned the racial tables in this instance because the Black man requested that the white woman abide by the rules. His schooling and his hobby already put Christian at odds with stereotypes of Black men. Dear Emmett, Black folk are deemed to be out of place in white spaces, and most public spaces where white folk go are immediately converted into white spaces, immediately become beachheads of white identity that honor and protect white views of how things should be. Christian's assertion of privilege, by requesting that Amy leash her dog, is unusual for Black folk. They are likely to simply leave white folk be even when they're breaking the rules. If Christian wasn't quite uppity, he was at least racially presumptuous by taking on a role white folk usually fill. Amy's unspoken white privilege was challenged, and her defensive behavior suggested her effort to regain the upper hand.

Christian further upset the racial applecart when he offered treats to Amy's dog to lure him out of the plant bed he was trampling. This is when Amy got angry and shifted into a more aggressive mode. After all, who was Christian to offer rewards to her dog and get him to disobey his master, his owner? It was then that Amy called the cops. She later admitted that she was "blessed" and that she had suddenly come to realize that she thinks of the cops as a "protection agency" and that other folk don't have that luxury. That much is true. Christian and his sister, Melody, who later posted the video to social media, knew that white women's tears have often been weaponized to bring down the wrath of the cops or other white men on the heads of Black men no matter their behavior or status. How many white lies have eased a noose around Black necks? It was great fortune that kept Christian, whose name means "follower of Christ," from being hurt by Amy, whose name means "beloved." In too many instances it takes an act of divine intervention to keep Black men from being the targets of revenge for allegedly harming beloved white women.

The Cooper encounter, which occurred on the same day as George Floyd's death, had a fortunate outcome, since no one was killed. Still, it added texture to our racial reckoning. In so many other cases the killings of Black folk caught on camera compose an eerie and horrifying cinema of Black death. Philosophers have spent more than a generation disputing the role of sight in arguments about knowledge and theories of truth. The optics of race are equally contentious and just as tricky when they reveal how Black folk are viewed on camera and in history. The development of new technology has permitted the truth of Black life to circulate far beyond our culture. This is particularly helpful when Black folk have had the nearly impossible task of convincing the world that what we say about how we are treated is true. Ahmaud's story and so many others bear brutal testimony to this undeniable reality. French scientist Philippe Kahn may have invented the camera phone in 1997 to share a photograph of his new baby daughter, but Black folk and many others have used the technology to help deliver a measure of justice to some of our babies after they have been savaged by the cops and vigilantes.

What we hear or see of race depends on who we are. There is little question that the mobile phone video recorder has effected a Gutenberg shift in the perception of race in America, although most of the recordings haven't yet resulted in structural change. But while this device, and social and traditional media too, permit us to see more of race, they may not necessarily help us to see race more clearly or deeply. We brag in some quarters about how young white folk will automatically see race in a far more enlightened fashion than their parents, and yet, with the exception of a greater acceptance of interracial intimacy, millennials see race in much the same way as white Generation Xers and baby boomers. The frustrating continuity on race between white generations suggests that it takes more than youth to conquer deeply entrenched beliefs. Those beliefs are hard to uproot even when they collide with novel or more nuanced images of Black identity. It is more difficult to reckon with race if we cannot agree on what we are seeing and what needs to be done to fix it.

Consider the case of Michael Brown, the unarmed teenager who was shot and killed by a white cop in the streets of Ferguson, Missouri, in 2014, sparking heated national protests. It was easier to believe that the video footage of Brown stealing cigarillos from a convenience store in the moments before his tragic death was more representative of his character as a "thug" than to believe that the recorded last gasps of Eric Garner in New York City claiming "I can't breathe" as he was choked to death by cops were the pleas of an unjustly accosted man. The video recording of Brown reinforced the belief that Black men are inherently criminal and therefore brutally policing them is acceptable. The Garner video reminded us that even an unarmed Black man begging to breathe is seen as untrustworthy. We cannot believe Garner's words because we have been taught to think of Black folk as incapable of telling the unbiased truth about race.

If we are to successfully reckon with race, we must understand the complexity and depth of what we see in racial terms. Race in America is not primarily about empirical proof of a given proposition — for instance, that Black folk are lazy, despise education, or are more violent than white folk. It is much more about the frameworks of perception that we are compelled to adopt to justify questionable or biased racial claims. Even when we add science to the mix, we don't necessarily reach a just or universally agreed-on conclusion. This is particularly true if the science we use has been shaped, for example, by deeply entrenched beliefs in the inherent inferiority of Black intelligence — beliefs that are in search of rational premises of support. In too many cases what we see is what we expect to see.

My dear Emmett, each time a new video surfaces of Black folk being murdered by their fellow citizens it recapitulates the sordid and tragic history of how Black folk have been seen in the culture. The video of unarmed Black motorist Walter Scott being murdered by white officer Michael Slager in South Carolina in April 2015 is instructive. Their brief but deadly encounter was captured on cellphone video: Slager drew his weapon and fired at the fleeing Scott eight times, dropping him dead in his tracks. Fortunately, and unusually, the video offered enough evidence to get Slager arrested. The Scott shooting occurred during yet another round of angry protests over a rash of Black bodies going down, from Michael Brown in Ferguson to Eric Garner in Staten Island. During a recent seven-year stretch ending in 2012 a white cop killed a Black person twice a week.

But to many outside the Black community, this only reinforced the belief that lethal force is often warranted when cops encounter "dangerous" Blacks. Such perceptions are slyly, and maliciously, validated when cops appeal to a common script, one deployed by Darren Wilson in Ferguson with Michael Brown, and by Slager before the recording of his encounter with Scott emerged: I was afraid for my life. The cultural bias against Black folk shapes the cops' narratives, which in turn bolster the prejudice from which those narratives borrow legitimacy. The stories these cops tell make sense to the white folk for whom they're crafted, including, beyond the general public, prosecutors, district attorneys, judges, and juries. The feedback loop is tight, and the circles in which the information is circulated are closely policed.

What looks obvious to Black folk is often seen as doubtful by many white folk. For decades, even centuries, Black folk have claimed that we are under siege by vigilantes and police forces. To many white eyes that claim looks exaggerated and suspicious. Our vastly different histories and divergent experiences shape our wildly competing visions of what is true and false. In many ways, we are constantly taking a racial Rorschach test. Even when it comes to seemingly flagrant examples of police misconduct there is often little consensus in the white world. Los Angeles motorist Rodney King was brutally beaten by four white cops in 1991, arguably the first such offense caught on a video recording, but a jury acquitted his abusers. Eric Garner pleaded for his life, but a grand jury failed to indict the cop who killed him. Black frustration mounts when Black folk have what they see as undeniable proof of police misconduct and yet it fails to move white folk to act.

As we reckon with the truths about race that have emerged since the nation began to pay serious attention, this truth must be remembered: when Black folk are not taken seriously, when we are routinely disbelieved, dismissed, or ridiculed for our effort to bear witness to our truths, it only increases the trauma we feel and increases our woeful vulnerability. The recording of Walter Scott being cut down was so terrifying because it was completely random. Is that not the point of terror, to make us all fear that any of us at any time might be its victim? I have said this before, in books, in sermons, in speeches, and in lectures, and it bears repeating here, again, because its truth is still not clear, my dear Emmett: to be Black in America is often to feel under siege, to feel, in the marrow of our bones, genuine terror. To feel that no matter how much education or money we have, how nice a car we drive, how well behaved we are, how disarming and articulate we prove ourselves to be, at any moment we might feel a baton crushing our skull, a Taser sending a jolting message to our nervous system, a bullet penetrating our flesh. All because, and for no other reason than, we are Black. That is terror, and, as I have said before, it comes in at least two speeds.

Slow terror is barely visible. It can't be easily detected because it is neither dramatic nor fussy, but it gets the job done beneath the skin. It may be masked, but it is no less malignant. Slow terror stalks Black bodies by denying us the sorts of opportunities at work or school that white folk take for granted. Slow terror bleeds into every crevice of Black existence. Slow terror causes Black boys and girls to be expelled from school at far higher rates than their white peers. Slow terror harasses Black men and women with unjust fines from local municipalities, as happened in Ferguson for decades. Slow terror drains billions of dollars of Black wealth, as happened during the mortgage crisis. And slow terror imprisons Black folk way out of proportion to our percentage in the population.

Fast terror is far more dynamic, far more clearly destructive, far more undeniably evident. Fast terror is the spectacle of Black death in public displays of vengeance and violence aimed at defenseless Black bodies, like that suffered by Ahmaud Arbery. Fast terror drops bombs and other incendiary devices on a Black community in Tulsa, Oklahoma, in 1921 in one of the earliest and most vicious acts of terror on American soil. Fast terror, my dear Emmett, lynched you and threw your mutilated body into the Tallahatchie River. Fast terror rapes, lynches, castrates, and drowns, achieving Black death in any way that's mean, nasty, heartless, or callous. Fast terror scares Black people; slow terror scars them.

The terror shows up, too, in the relentless bombardment of Black folk with grief and thoughts and fears of death. Black kids with death on their minds don't perform as well as they might otherwise do in the classroom. Black youth with death on their brains find other sorts of bedlam to blunt the pain, or, tragically, they duplicate the trauma of loss by causing more death. These youth realize they are but a corpse in the making, an autopsy short of hitting the gruesome trifecta in too much of Black life: targeted by cops, tagged by coroners, and treasured by loved ones, or — if their bad luck turned to posthumous renown — by a Black public that sees itself in their deaths. These young folk are made martyrs before their time, before they could take time to become who they were meant to be, or might have become, had they lived past their youthful experiments and indiscretions like millions of white kids who live to tell about it after they become artists, or writers, or gurus, or inventors, or business giants, or television stars, or president.

Black parents, wives, husbands, other relatives and loved ones with death on their minds become caretakers of ordinary bodies that sometimes in death gather extraordinary legacies. They are hard-pressed to reveal their fallen kin's redeeming features without surrendering to the pressure for Black victims to be perfect. Yet they need to show and tell how their loved ones deserved to live out their days like everyone else without having to prove that they were the next great anything or the next remarkable someone. That is why the claims that grew out of cultural and political movements for Black self-recognition felt so true for millions of Black folk: "Black is beautiful" rang out in the sixties, "I am somebody" echoed in the seventies, and "Black lives matter" resonates in our day. More than slogans or hashtags, these are verbal efforts to stave off the terror of dead Black bodies. Please remember that, white brothers and sisters, the next time one of your friends argues that "all lives matter."

We can see how slow and fast terror, sometimes separated, sometimes carelessly intermingled, played out in Ferguson, Missouri, before and after the Michael Brown shooting. It is not difficult to understand how Ferguson fatally combusted into screeching chaos: several decades of aggressive and intemperate policing; the repeated slaughter of unarmed Black folk; the unspeakable poverty of Black citizens; the unyielding bias and deeply rooted racism in the criminal justice system and other societal institutions; the astonishing and persistent social inequality; the rampant disenfranchisement of large pockets of Black communities; and an unreliable escalator to upward mobility that grew shakier by the day. Michael Brown's killing showed the stakes for Black youth in a culture that both despises and fears them. His death at the hands of officer Darren Wilson was clearly an example of fast terror. The six-foot-four-inch, 210-pound Wilson claimed that his encounter with the six-foot-four-inch, 292-pound Brown made him feel like "a five-year-old holding on to Hulk Hogan." Wilson revealed his beliefs about Brown's lack of humanity when he used the impersonal pronoun "it" to describe how Brown looked like a "demon" rushing him. Many Black folk felt that Brown's stature offered him a fighter's chance in a brutal encounter with a cop who claimed that he tussled with the youth, first inside his car as Brown reached in to punch him, and then on the pavement as Wilson struggled out of his car to give chase. But Wilson shot the teenager six times. The first five shots, a private autopsy found, Brown might have survived, but it was the last shot, to the top of his head, that killed him. To the cop and many whites, Brown was the burly Black menace come to life, the terrorizing monster who haunts the white imagination. These conflicting perceptions highlight a different aspect of the physics of race, where an observer effect prevails: the instrument of racial perception, whether it is one's experiences, one's fears or fantasies, or one's culture, profoundly alters what it measures.

Before the recent spate of cellphone videos of Black folk perishing at the hands of cops and others, there were hardly any moving images of Black death. There have always been stories, testimonies, claims, and arguments, of course, but the recordings capture indisputable proof of Black death having actually occurred as Black folk said it did. The process by which older cameras captured their images offer a compelling metaphor for how the photograph — unlike the video image — may obscure as much as it reveals. There was something in the very visual language of the photograph that seemed to conspire metaphorically against Black being. The camera's framing of Black bodies through its lens suggested how so many Black bodies were framed by whiteness in a culture that disdained the very image of Blackness.

The photographs of lynching parties came closest to reflecting the joy the white world felt about Black death. To extend the metaphor: just as a photograph is produced from a negative, the negative forces in Black life often helped to produce a portrait of our culture and condition. The camera's exposure suggested our very vulnerability. Black folk, even great Black folk, had the aftermath of their violent death captured and stilled by that camera's frozen-in-time snapshot. Snap. Shot. The photograph is itself an autopsy of time and space, a convergence of the seen and unseen, a record of what might be witnessed. A photograph makes sacred the visible, renders holy the seen. The vast unseen is the backdrop for what is witnessed, the basis of being able to see at all.

My dear Emmett, the siege of Black death at the hands of our fellow citizens and by nature's fury has brought the nation to its collective senses. Rarely has the tragic fact of Black death been as urgently in need of interpretation and engagement as in this moment. America has been trying for a couple of centuries now to reconcile its self-image as a shining beacon of democracy with the nation's corrupted and unjust practices. We have promised time and again to change from within, motivated by some crisis, moved by some uprising, shamed by some catastrophe that wore on our consciences. But each time we bowed to the inertia brought on by half-hearted half measures. Something feels different now, but how far are we willing to go? Are we prepared to sacrifice tradition and convention for genuine transformation? Are we ready to reckon with the disastrous social forces that have been unleashed in such unprecedented fashion? Time alone will not tell; our commitment to change how we see Black bodies will, and so will our determination to keep the forces called to serve us from killing those we have too often left unprotected.

I looked and I saw
That man they call the Law.
He was coming
Down the street at me!
I had visions in my head
Of being laid out cold and dead,
Or else murdered
By the third degree.
— LANGSTON HUGHES,
"WHO BUT THE LORD?"

# 2. BLUE PLAGUE

Dear Eric Garner,

I must say, my friend, I can barely begin to understand how we are back here again, back to a Black man begging to breathe as the cops kill him. As if your death wasn't tragic enough. As if your death hadn't sent so many of us into the streets to protest the horrors of what we saw when you were suffocated in broad daylight. As if your death hadn't already proved the meanness and heartlessness of a police force that has sought to asphyxiate our bodies and drain them of life and blood. As if your death hadn't already made us feel utterly endangered and defenseless in the face of cops who will never respect us or treat us like their kin.

But you were our kin. When most of us Black folk saw you, we recognized you. We knew the kind of brother you were. The kind who would do anything for his family to make sure they had a roof over their heads and food on the table. The kind who would hustle in the street and dip into the underground economy to make sure you didn't go home empty-handed. And what's a brother like you to do? The educational system has little regard for fellows like you. I've seen it up close. Black male styles of learning are sometimes too irregular, too off the charts, too aggressive, for the teachers and school officials who can't handle our energy. We are not always linear, we don't always color inside the lines, but we are good folk nonetheless.

You remind me of my brother Everett. He went much further in the underground economy than you. He actually took to the streets and sold drugs until he was arrested for the murder of a good man who was also an alleged drug dealer. I always believed Everett was innocent, not because he was my brother but because the evidence never stacked up. Mostly there was no evidence at all except the dying man's words about a killer whose name sounded something like my brother's. That was all it took to get him convicted before an all-Black jury and locked away for thirty years until he died in prison a couple of years ago. It hurt to visit him under those circumstances. He always

had a good word to say; he was always reading, studying, trying to figure a way out of
the hellhole he lived in for three decades
even as he consistently maintained his innocence. He refused to make a false confes-
sion, which would have made it easier for
him to get out of prison, but he never
wavered in telling me he didn't do it and he
wasn't going to lie about it just to get out. I
admired him for that decision, but it was
hard to watch him stay cooped up in that
cage.

I know you had been arrested several
times, mostly for selling unlicensed cigarettes. How many brothers are doing the
same, or, like Alton Sterling, selling bootleg
CDs and DVDs, trying to make ends meet
and trying, as the rapper 2Pac said, to
"make a dollar out of fifteen cents"? Like
my brother, you were a big man, except you
were even bigger, and when you're a big
Black man they fear you before they hear
you — "they" being so many cops who
deem themselves street tough. They resent
you for no other reason than you're big,
Black, and breathing. There's something
strange that Black men of a certain girth
and width and build and presence do to the
mindset of white cops who take it person-
ally that you're constructed as you are, and

they deem it their mission to handle you, to control you, and to take you down, if necessary, like they did to you on the streets of Staten Island.

When they made you beg for your life it broke my heart. Anyone could see that you were hardly a menace. Anybody could see that you were a gentle giant. Just like George Floyd. It is because of men like you, ordinary, everyday Black folk who are wasted as you try to do the best you can, that we must reckon with the plague of police brutality and how it has ravaged Black communities for three centuries. The cops remain in large part violent enforcers of white supremacy. The untold devastation of the blue plague can hardly be captured in videos of Black men and women dying at the hands of cops. As horrifying as these recordings are, they are but the tip of a destructive iceberg of violence and death lodged beneath the ocean of Black existence, wrecking many a life. For this reason, grappling with the police and how they see and treat Black folk is a central imperative of national reckoning. If our bodies are not alive and free from brutality and the repeated efforts to kill us, there can be no reckoning with any other facet of systemic racism. In order for systems of oppression to be reformed, or discarded, or abolished, Black bodies must be present and breathing.

My brother Eric, to see the parallels between you and George Floyd is to see that no matter how much we said we had progressed in this nation, Black bodies are still an object of scorn and aversion. Black bodies are still an object of nearly unconscious rage that rattles the cavernous egos of some men who think themselves mighty because they sport a badge and a gun and have referred swagger. That's the sort of swagger that doesn't draw from their innate charisma. Instead it is a forced appeal that derives from the hardware they wear, or really, in truth, the hardware that wears them, their flesh an emblem of the license to kill that brings a lot of them such perverse joy. The cop who killed George Floyd didn't look sad. His demeanor stoic, his hand in his pocket, he seemed to gain a ghastly satisfaction the longer he depressed George's mortally bruised collum.

Dear brother Eric, the circumstances of your death were awful enough. But George's death played out against the backdrop of a global pandemic and its wickedly calamitous romp through Black America. On the one hand, COVID-19 decimates Black communities. On the other hand, George's death underscores the harrowing legacy of white supremacy donning the gear of a state patrol or a city cop. The dual pandemics tear into the bodies of Black folk and often leave us gasping for air. They are a perfect analogy for each other: police are the pandemic's deadly effects colored blue, and the pandemic is a metaphor for how cops often maliciously will Black bodies dead.

The pandemic also urged us to another level of metaphor as it forced us inside our homes while forcing us deeper inside ourselves, deeper inside our thoughts about how we have lived, and deeper inside habits of mind or spirit that have nourished or harmed us. Instead of the immediacy of seeing each other in the flesh, we have had to settle, paradoxically enough, for the remote intimacy of screens. Because we have all grown accustomed to blurred images, faulty transmissions, and other technological hiccups, suddenly an imperfect image was no longer a bother to purists who a short while earlier had demanded high definition or bust.

When images of George Floyd lying on the ground and pleading for his life flooded our screens, we had already adjusted our expectations of what lived experience was like. With our senses heightened, we could nearly taste and touch what we were forced to see at a distance. We were able, without the aid of technology, to add textures and colors to what we see, as we split the difference between memory and imagination. Floyd's face, jammed beneath the cop's knee, was more vivid to us than what the video allowed, his cries amplified beyond his voice's muffled volume, his moans and pleas carrying a greater poignancy than the medium alone might convey. We saw him, yes, but we felt him even more. We were more than literally there; we were morally and spiritually there. We were fatally wedged with him beneath the weight of a death-dealing cop as George begged for his life. His only defense was his utter defenselessness, but in order for that to work, in order for his defenselessness to matter, that cop would have to have a sense of morality and to see Floyd as a human being. Neither, sadly, was the case, my brother Eric.

The pandemic forced more of us to be home at the same time to watch our screens and to be sickened and angered at the treatment of Floyd's helpless body. In that sense, the origin of our reckoning was a made-for-social-media event, a species of digital disruption that forced us to stream the truth of Black suffering and national crisis as we were left to our own devices. The pandemic made it easier to absorb his tragically prostrate form into the national conscience. Many white people gained empathy when they realized that Black folk were already suffering more than others from COVID-19. But those same white folk were surprised by what Black folk already knew: not even a pandemic that was supposed to unite us could halt the massacre of Black bodies by the cops. The new white empathy took political shape too, and for a fleeting moment there weren't white or Black screens, just American screens. Blackness had chanced on the sort of universality that only whiteness has historically enjoyed. The video recording of Floyd's death broke our hearts and merged them all at once. That surely made this death different from so many other Black deaths. Was this finally the moment we would be done with our passive support for change and move into the active voice of resistance?

Still, my brother Eric, it is not as if we hadn't literally seen this movie before. The recording of your gasping for air and claiming eleven times "I can't breathe" set off broad Black mobilization and social unrest six years ago, in July 2014, when your big

Black body lay limp on the ground for seven minutes after the cop killed you and before the ambulance arrived. But that's just it: while Floyd's death undeniably seized the nation's awareness and shook its conscience like never before, it surely didn't come out of nowhere. It was preceded by too many Black deaths to name, too many Black deaths to absorb, too many Black deaths to remember, too many Black deaths to account for, too many Black deaths to obsess over. Forcing Black folk to obsess over death saps our power and distracts us from the full pursuit of life. In the wake of such an obsession, Black life slowly and imperceptibly ebbs away, slipping through the cracks while hardly anyone beyond our culture pays attention.

The names of the victims of the blue plague whose last moments are caught on camera — Tamir Rice, Philando Castile, Alton Sterling, Walter Scott, Laquan McDonald, George Floyd, and you, brother Eric — are a roll call of urban Black heroism, a list of souls crushed into sainthood by the forces of evil, a ritual of sacred Black transubstantiation that turns their bodies from flesh and blood to holy hashtags and metaphysical martyrs for justice. How many times have we watched Black folk die at the hands of cops who are not held accountable or who even reenact their heinous acts while mugging for the camera? Much like a Hollywood film franchise, the on-camera violence of cops harming Blacks is haunted by sequels: the locations may change, the actors are different, but the story remains the same.

Police dominating Black life is a long-standing and heartily endorsed practice that traces back to slavery. White fear of Black bodies goes back to the plantation and fuels the rise of the modern white cop. Police channel the white desire to inspect, control, and literally arrest Black aspiration. If southern white cops in the sixties brutalized Black bodies in the heat of the night, northern white cops beat them into submission in the light of day. The state's efforts to govern Black bodies, society's desire to control Black mobility, and the criminal justice system's will to outlaw and contain Black danger all came to rest on the cop's shoulders. The police officer is the most visible and accessible representative of the state that most Black folk encounter. He zealously protects and proudly serves white society. He eagerly executes swift and often fatal judgment on vulnerable Black bodies. The most innocuous interaction with cops can quickly turn dangerous. A consensual encounter, a routine traffic stop, a minor sidewalk dispute — all can end in Black death. The recent videos of Black folk perishing at the hands of cops compose the lurid pornography of Black death.

What is clear, too, is that the cops are often needlessly disrespectful, that they despise our skin and breath, that they rain down on our bodies waves of gratuitous violence, that they have no regard at all for our safety and protection, that our lives matter so little to them that it makes no difference if they execute a warrant or our flesh. The toll of bodies randomly recited is astonishing and dispiriting. Walter E. Brown was shot by two white cops in New Orleans in 1980 for cursing at them. Although the cops resigned after confessing that they had planted a gun on Brown, a grand jury later concluded they had done nothing wrong. That same year, Cornelius Brown, a forty-two-year-old Black man from Cleveland, was shot four times and killed by an off-duty white cop wielding a .38 caliber weapon, angry that Brown remained at a delicatessen after he demanded that Brown leave. The cop lied and accused Brown of attempting to attack him with a pool cue, a story the jury believed, clearing the way for the cop to rejoin the force. Twenty-year-old Theodoric Johnson was chased down in Roseville, Michigan, in 1981 by two cops who mistakenly believed he and his two compatriots had stolen a car, after which they shot and killed him; one cop bragged to his colleague, "I blew that nigger's head off." In 1981, Leroy Perry, a forty-eight-year-old Black man from Annapolis, Maryland, was stopped by a white cop for suspected drunk driving, and when he retrieved a screwdriver to open the trunk where he kept his registration, the cop shot and killed him. So many other names, too many other names, can be added to the list.

It wasn't any better in the nineties and aughts. In December 1990, in Minneapolis, Minnesota, seventeen-year-old Tycel Nelson was chased down and shot in the back and killed by a cop wielding a shotgun. The officer wasn't charged in Tycel's death — and was later awarded his department's medal of valor for his bravery in gunning him down. He returned the medal in response to community outrage. In December 1998, Tyisha Shenee Miller, a Black woman from Rubidoux, California, was shot and killed by police officers after her family called the authorities because they couldn't awaken her as she lay unconscious in a car. In Los

Angeles in 1999, a five-foot-one homeless and mentally ill widow named Margaret Mitchell was shot to death by a police officer while waving a screwdriver after she was stopped on suspicion of stealing a shopping cart. That same year, in Chicago, when a driver fled a police traffic stop, the cops gave chase for thirty-one blocks, after which a police officer shot and killed a passenger in the car, twenty-six-year-old LaTanya Haggerty, mistaking her cellphone for a weapon. The cop knelt on the sidewalk next to Haggerty, placed a leather coat beneath her head, stroked her blood-soaked hair, and confessed, "I'm sorry. I didn't mean to shoot you. I thought you had a gun." While she and two other cops were fired because they ignored orders and unloaded on Haggerty without justification, none of them were prosecuted. In 2000, in Minneapolis, the cops shot and killed mentally ill Alfred "Abuka" Sanders, twenty-nine, firing thirty-three rounds of ammunition and striking his body at least sixteen times. He was unarmed and had committed no crime.

Other Black bodies succumbed to the blue plague too, including women whose deaths are not as often the object of national outrage or intense debate. In Oregon in 2003, Kendra James, a mother of two, was killed after a cop put a gun to her head inside a car during a traffic stop. He claimed the vehicle then moved, and, supposedly fearing what might happen to him, he fired a single shot into her skull. Kathryn Johnston, a ninety-two-year-old Black woman from Atlanta, Georgia, was killed in 2006 by undercover cops during yet another botched drug raid. They cut off her burglar bars and broke down her door on a no-knock warrant; as they entered, she fired a single shot over the cops' heads, and they returned fire, aiming thirty-nine shots at her, five or six of which found their target in her elderly body. In 2008, during a raid in Lima, Ohio, that targeted her boyfriend, who was suspected of being a drug dealer, twenty-six-year-old Tarika Wilson, sheltering in her bedroom with her six children, was killed when a cop shot blindly into the room. He killed her instantly and injured the baby in her arms. Later her son had to have his finger amputated.

In the last decade alone, besides you, brother Eric, and others I've mentioned, the names of the lost are legion. Rekia Boyd. John Crawford III. Ezell Ford. Dante Parker. Michelle Cusseaux. Tanisha Anderson. Akai Gurley. Rumain Brisbon. Jerame Reid. George Mann. Matthew Ajibade.

Frank Smart. Natasha McKenna. Tony Robinson. Anthony Hill. Mya Hall. Phillip White. Eric Harris. William Chapman II. Alexia Christian. Brendon Glenn. Victor Manuel Larosa. Jonathan Sanders. Freddie Gray. Freddie Blue. Joseph Mann. Salvado Ellswood. Sandra Bland. Danroy Henry. Albert Joseph Davis. Darrius Stewart. Bill Ray Davis. Samuel Dubose. Michael Sabbie. Brian Keith Day. Christian Taylor. Troy Robinson. Asshams Pharoah Manley. Felix Kumi. Keith Harrison McLeod. Junior Prosper. Lamontez Jones. Paterson Brown. Dominic Hutchinson. Anthony Ashford. Alonzo Smith. Tyree Crawford. India Kager. La'Vante Biggs. Michael Lee Marshall. Jamar Clark. Richard Perkins. Nathaniel Harris Pickett. Bennie Lee Tignor. Miguel Espinal. Michael Noel. Kevin Matthews. Bettie Jones. Quintonio Legrier. Keith Childress Jr. Janet Wilson. Randy Nelson. Antronie Scott. Wendell Celestine. David Joseph. Calin Roquemore. Dyzhawn Perkins. Christopher Davis. Marco Loud. Peter Gaines. Torrey Robinson. Darius Robinson. Kevin Hicks. Mary Truxillo. DeMarcus Semer. Willie Tillman. Terrill Thomas. Sylville Smith. Terence Crutcher. Paul O'Neal. Alteria Woods. Jordan Edwards. Aaron Bailey. Ronell Foster. Stephon Clark. Antwon Rose

77

II. Botham Jean. Pamela Turner. Dominique Clayton. Atatiana Jefferson. Christopher Whitfield. Christopher McCorvey. Eric Reason. Michael Lorenzo Dean. Breonna Taylor. Yes, my friends of every race, in your heads or gently on your lips, say their names in a litany of remembrance.

Brother Eric, each of these precious women and men, including you, each of these beautiful boys and girls added to the gallery of grief that gripped the collective Black soul. Each death extended the centuries-long assault by the police on Black safety and welfare. Each death haunted the racial geography and moral psychology of Black America. Each of these deaths imposed brutal punishment on our increasingly fractured psyches. If we picture the impact of each of these losses on Black America as a punch in a prizefight, then each of these deaths was a body blow to Black justice. Each shooting was a stinging jab to our spirits. Each killing was a right cross to our emotional stability. Each choking was a left hook to our concerted efforts to push ahead. And then, after all those years, after all this incalculable loss, the knockout punch was a bruising uppercut to our minds delivered as George Floyd's coldly brutal death.

Floyd's death was arguably the most affecting murder by a cop that we have witnessed in the homemade cinema of Black death. It was the unsettling and sordid drama of it all that got to us, the way it played out on our screens as deadly suspense clashing with chilling horror.

The saga begins in eerie ordinariness on a Monday evening in late May 2020. The police are summoned to a grocery store on East 38th Street and Chicago Avenue in South Minneapolis because a man has allegedly used a fake twenty-dollar bill to purchase cigarettes, a twenty that the owner later admits that George, like most customers, may not even have realized was fake. Forty-six-year-old George Floyd was a six-foot-six Black man, a gregarious soul and gentle giant who often brought life to the circles in which he traveled and was considered a "king" by some of his friends. This made it even more tragic, given the tough subcultures he had survived, to have his life end in pitiless submission to a man he could have easily thrashed had this been a fair fight. Such conflicts between Black and white men are invariably tinged with psychosexual jealousy. Many white men arm themselves to the teeth to subdue the massive Black manhood that they have been led to believe that they could never best in the sack, in sports, or in the streets. George's size and rich dark skin capture that fraught history in every inch of his well-built frame. We could not get a true measure of his impressive physical presence as he lay stretched out on the ground. And that, in part, was the point, is always the point when Black men who ride high for no other reason than the confident possession of their bodies are brought low. The humiliating actions of brutal white cops toward Black men are ritual castrations of a seminal but threatening Black masculinity.

Floyd had put his big Black body to good use as a bouncer in Minneapolis after he escaped his native Houston, where his hustling led to nine arrests, mostly for drug and theft charges, and where, before that, he was a star high school football and basketball player. (Even before that, as a second-grade student, George was inspired by the example of Thurgood Marshall and wrote in an assignment, "I want to be a Supreme Court Judge." The tragedy of his unjust death increases the sad irony of the eight-year-old boy's dream.) Floyd lost his job because of the pandemic.

That May evening as he sits in the driver's seat of a blue Mercedes SUV across the street from Cup Foods, Floyd and the two other folk in his car — his ex-girlfriend Shawanda Hill in the backseat and his longtime friend Maurice Lester Hall on the passenger side — are confronted by a couple of store employees. After Floyd refuses their demand to give the cigarettes back, the Cup Foods employees call the cops about the shady transaction and report that Floyd is drunk and not in control of himself. Shortly thereafter officers Thomas Lane and J. Alexander Kueng arrive on the scene and speak to the store clerks, who direct them across the street to Floyd's car while imploring them to catch the suspects before they peel off.

Lane and Kueng carefully approach Floyd's car. On the driver's side Lane quickly pulls his gun and orders Floyd to put his hands on the wheel. Almost from the start Lane escalates the situation and Floyd is nervous, perhaps having had enough experience to warrant a general Black anxiety around cops. Lane snaps at him a few times, frustrated that he is not obeying to his liking.

"Put your fucking hands up right now!"

Lane says, his obscenity suggesting he means business. "Let me see your other hand."

"Let him see your other hand," Hill says, repeating Lane's order.

"All right. What I do, though? What we do, Mr. Officer?" Floyd pleads. Of course, Lane ignores him.

"Put your hand up there. Put your fucking hand up there! Jesus Christ, keep your fucking hands on the wheel."

Lane grows more agitated. Floyd tells him he's been shot before, making the sort of small talk that is meant, perhaps, to establish empathy, to make himself seem less threatening. Brother Eric, you knew this well: big Black men are used to making such concessions and issuing such reassurances to put folk at ease, especially white folk, and even more so with white folk in authority. After Floyd identifies the two other people in the car for Lane, he sticks his foot out the door, foreshadowing his subsequent claim to be spooked by cramped spaces.

"Put your foot back in!" Lane yells.

"I'm sorry. I'm so sorry. God dang, man. Man, I got . . . shot the same way, Mr. Officer, before."

"Okay," Lane says, seeming to calm down a bit, only to fling another obscenity at

George. "Well, when I say, 'Let me see your hands,' you put your fucking hands up." After Lane put his gun back in the holster, having gone back and forth with Floyd for a minute and a half, he suddenly yanks him from the car.

Meanwhile, in a nod to the belief that every interaction with the cops should be recorded, since they often do wrong and cause harm, a man in a car parked behind Floyd's vehicle begins filming the encounter on his phone. That is when Floyd makes a plea, a plea on most Black folk's minds when stopped by the cops.

"Okay, Mr. Officer, please don't shoot me. Please, man."

"I'm not going to shoot you," Lane assures him. "Step out and face away."

As Floyd repeatedly begs the cops not to shoot him and grows more anxious, Hill tells him to stop resisting. When the cops explain that there has been a report of a fake bill being passed, Floyd tells them directly: "I'm scared, man." Then Lane and Kueng cuff his hands behind his back and Kueng makes him sit down on the sidewalk away from his car. Even though the convenience store workers told the police he was drunk and out of control, Floyd is peaceful and certainly not abrasive or violent. But he does appear already to be in no small amount of distress.

About six minutes into their encounter, the cops decide to take Floyd back to their car. As they get close to the cruiser, Floyd suddenly falls to the ground, telling them that he is claustrophobic. He repeatedly asks to explain his phobia. But the cops insist that he follow their orders and get in the car. Floyd says he will. But even though Lane says he'll roll the windows down, Floyd can't bring himself to get in. His claustrophobia appears real. It's easy to see how his six-foot-six frame could feel out of sorts in the back of their vehicle. Floyd struggles with the cops and repeatedly tells them that he is scared and doesn't want to get shot. And not too long before he ends up on the ground, he says he can't breathe. Floyd tells them, "Y'all, I'm going to die in here! I'm going to die, man!"

Nine minutes into his arrest, after a second police vehicle had already arrived, a third cop car, containing officers Tou Thao and Derek Chauvin, pulls up. That is certainly bad news, since Thao has had six complaints against him, including a brutality lawsuit three years earlier for throwing a man to the ground and assaulting him. Chauvin is even more accomplished in blue mayhem; he's drawn seventeen complaints and been involved in three shootings, one of them fatal. Chauvin, true to form, immediately joins the effort to force Floyd into the vehicle. Then Kueng struggles with him in the backseat as he repeatedly proclaims his claustrophobia. As they attempt to subdue him, Floyd says he wants to lie on the ground rather than be cramped inside the car. Chauvin then violently yanks him out of the backseat and pushes him face-down in the street.

At this point, two additional witnesses begin filming the escalating incident with their phones. From the angle of one camera, situated in the street, we see that Chauvin has his knee on Floyd's neck, Kueng is resting his knees on Floyd's torso, and Lane is holding down George's legs with his knees. Thao serves as a complicit lookout, a sentinel to protect his brothers in arms from being interrupted in the execution of their duties, and eventually, tragically, in the execution of Floyd.

"Ah ha," Floyd cries out. "I can't breathe, man. Please."

It is painful, my brother Eric, to hear a grown man cry like that. George remains respectful even as their knees bore into his outstretched body. The person filming from

85

the street is waved off by Lane. But on the sidewalk, seventeen-year-old Darnella Frazier courageously keeps recording. Now the cops call in a code 2, for nonemergency medical assistance, because of an injury to Floyd's mouth. On the radio transmission you can hear Floyd pleading and struggling in the background, even as the call is quickly upgraded to a code 3, for emergency medical assistance. Frazier's camera records Chauvin digging his knee into Floyd's neck for at least another eight minutes despite the emergency call for help. An unsettling horror unfolds before our very eyes.

"What do you want?" an irritated Chauvin demands.

"I can't breathe," Floyd begs him. "Please, the knee in my neck. I can't breathe. Shit."

Then what sounds like a Black male voice rings out from the sidewalk, inexplicably demanding: "Well, get up, get in the car, man."

"I will," George replies desperately.

"Get up and get in the car."

"I can't move."

"I been watching the whole thang, man."

"Aaaa haaaa," Floyd cries out again.

"Get up and get in the car."

"Mama," Floyd cries.

"Get up . . ."

"Mama!"

". . . and get in the car, right . . ."

"I can't."

This man interjects the Theater of the Absurd into Floyd's tragic drama. But this sidewalk Samuel Beckett lacks the poetry of the master. Still, the absurdity feels familiar: the impossible choices that Black folk face, one of us pinned beneath the knee of a cop that he clearly can't escape, and the other, perhaps a friend or some well-meaning bystander, pinned down by the depressingly familiar lack of choices that all too frequently limit Black life. Perhaps the man is speaking as much to Chauvin as to Floyd, afraid to anger the cop further by addressing him directly, not wanting to embarrass Chauvin by pointing out how clearly inhumane and evil his actions are, thus risking him only getting more ornery. It was his way of saying, "I see the right in what you requested of George, and by suggesting that, accept my plea for him to get up as a substitute acknowledgment that he was wrong and you were right, but please don't make him pay for this mistake with his life." The man may have been acting as Floyd's representative, a sidewalk lawyer of sorts, since the cops are clearly meting out their own brand of justice. He couldn't directly cross-examine them, so he speaks to, and through, Floyd. When the choice is between the anxiety of claustrophobia and not breathing at all, Floyd wants to live and breathe.

Brother Eric, Floyd's calling out for his recently deceased mother is especially hard to hear. Mothers are broadly cherished in this country, but Black mothers have a special magical place in Black culture. When he cries "Mama," he is crying out for his maternal root, his most loving supporter, his first and foremost advocate and protector. And how he needs her now to protect him, a six-foot-six Black man who weathered jail and the streets, now lying on one of them, its pavement a harsh pillow and the concrete a pallet of pain that will soon be his temporary cooling board. Black mothers are totemic in Black life. Calling out for his mother means that Floyd needs the woman who brought him into the world to watch over him, and increasingly, as it becomes apparent to him that he might not make it, he needs her to ferry him into eternity to join her. Compressed into the cry for his mother is the recognition that so many Black mothers have been mother and then so much more. The incantatory power lies in merely calling out for her. In Black life, the title "Mama" conjures a vast world of competences and habits, skills and outlooks, loves, loves, and more loves, of magnitudes far beyond what any words might capture. The very cry for her is enough to communicate the trouble at hand, the desperation being expressed, the love that is needed. It is all rolled into that single word, and when it is uttered under such pressure and pain, it draws on an inexhaustible reservoir of care. Floyd's crying out for his mother struck a nerve in the millions who heard him.

"Mama, Mama, Mama, Mama," Floyd cries out again. And again, and again, and again, and again, and again. More than ten times. He calls her name in wild and repeated disbelief.

"I can't believe this, man. Mom. I love you."

At another time, he confesses his helplessness to her, as if he were somehow disappointing her by not being able to get up. How many times have we heard stories in Black life where the narrator recalls how he got beat up in his ghetto neighborhood, and instead of his mother or father allowing him to come home crying and be consoled, the parent sent him back to the street to fight his assailant or else face a beating at home?

It's as if George were apologizing for not being able to heave his mighty physique at the cops and beat them down.

"Mama, I love you. I can't do nothing."

Floyd has already acknowledged the immoral character of the cops assaulting him.

"I can't breathe or nothing, man. This cold-blooded." Then he lets out another rush of bloodcurdling cries. "Ah-ah! Ah-ah! Ah-ah!" The gut-wrenching trio of exclamations rips the soul with their utter desperation.

Right on cue, the dispassionate and soulless Chauvin can't help but confirm how flip he is: "You're doing a lot of talking, man."

Later, Kueng pipes up: "You're fine, you're talking fine." This is especially tragic coming from the lips of a Black cop who is just three shifts into a job he took in large measure to protect Black people from the kind of disaster that is unfolding beneath his very knees. Kueng heaps insult upon the injury to Floyd by at one point asking Lane if he is good. "My knee might be a little scratched, but I'll survive," Lane responds without a hint of irony. Things get more twisted when Chauvin acerbically offers further advice to Floyd: "Then stop talking, stop yelling. It takes a heck of a lot of oxygen to talk."

"I can't fucking breathe," Floyd cries out again and again and again and again and again and again and again. More than twenty times.

They won't listen, brother Eric, just as the cops didn't listen to you. They won't hear him. And Chauvin, with casual coldness, sticks his hand in his pocket, both signifying his absolute indifference to George's plight and putting additional pressure on his neck. Chauvin's actions echo Hannah Arendt's notion of the "banality of evil." The unremarkable everydayness with which he does his job fails to mask its astonishing moral corruption. Chauvin and Lane are whiteness's punishing representatives, while Thao and Kueng serve as honorary members of the tribe.

Floyd desperately shouts out the parts of his body. This harkens back to dehumanizing chattel slavery, where every part of the body had to be accountable and subservient to the white world. George is reminded that he owns nothing. Not even his life or death. All of that is decided for him. "My face is gone," he says. "My face is getting it bad." And later, "My stomach hurts. My neck hurts. Everything hurts." Meanwhile, Lane and the others discuss Floyd's body as if it is an anthropological artifact.

Floyd, as did Martin Luther King, presents an automortology, the narration of one's own death, a kind of speech that hovers in the future while, from that vantage point, looking back to what is actually the present, to the fact of one's death. Floyd, in effect, offers for himself an announcement of his death ("I'm dead"), a farewell to loved ones ("Tell my kids I love them"), describing the symptom of his death ("I can't breathe"), the means of his death ("Please, the knee in my neck . . . I'll probably just die this way"), the perpetrators of his death ("Why y'all doing me like this, Mr. Officer?"), and their conscious intent to kill him ("They'll kill me"). Time and again he tells the officers that he is slipping away right beneath their knees. In staring his own death in the face, Floyd utters his last words, as another martyr, Jesus, did from the cross — or, in Floyd's case, the pavement.

Jesus's seven last sayings were memorialized in scripture. Jesus's first saying was, "Father, forgive them; for they know not what they do." The closest Floyd came to that was telling the cops, "I'll do anything y'all tell me to, man . . . You can ask him,

92

they know me." George's extreme deference expressed a desire to get out of the encounter alive. It also expressed a graciousness that was a kind of forgiveness of the cops, a willingness to put himself in their shoes and imagine what they might feel. That is perhaps why he told Lane early in their encounter that he too knew what it felt like to be shot. Jesus's second saying was "Today you will be with me in paradise," referring to the thief on the cross who died with him that day and asked to be remembered by Jesus when he came into God's kingdom. Floyd pleaded, too: "Oh man, God, don't leave me, man. Please, man, please, man . . . Don't leave me by myself, man."

Jesus's third saying was "Woman, behold, thy son! Behold, thy mother!" George cries out, "Mama, Mama, Mama." He calls for his mother nearly a dozen times and pledges his love for her, even telling the cops that he has just lost his mom. Jesus's fourth saying was, "My God, my God, why hast thou forsaken me?" Floyd comes close to this in his last words, resorting to a grassroots theology of suffering, a homegrown theodicy that grappled with what should not occur in a just world. "God, man . . . Why is this going on like this?" Floyd asks. "Oh my God. I can't believe this. I can't believe this." Jesus's fifth saying from the cross was composed of two words: "I thirst." George declares, "I need some water or something, please." Jesus's sixth saying was, "It is finished." Floyd simply says, "I'm through, I'm through." The seventh and final saying from the cross was Jesus crying out in a loud voice, "Father, into thy hands I commend my spirit." Floyd doesn't audibly place his spirit in God's hands, though his faith suggests he would have. But Floyd did, several times, cry out in a loud voice, and as the Word says, his groans would be interpreted by the Spirit.

Jesus had a few folks gathered around the cross when he died. So did George Floyd. One of the witnesses was Donald Williams, a brave young Black man who commented in a bracing minutes-long soliloquy for Chauvin to get his knee off Floyd; that the cop was a "bum" and that he was trying to prove he was "tough"; that, as a practitioner of martial arts, Williams was familiar with the "blood choke" that Chauvin was using (a stranglehold that stops the flow of blood to the brain); and that the cop was going to kill Floyd. Williams's needling drew a brief defensive response from the cops. But Williams was unrelenting; he repeatedly pleaded with them to check George's pulse. So did twenty-eight-year-old white rookie fire-fighter Genevieve Hansen. Like Williams, she resorted to expletives to urge the cops to do the right thing. "What the fuck?" she chided them in anxious disbelief. She tried to get closer to Floyd to check on him, but she was warned to keep away by Chauvin, Lane, and Kueng. She identified herself as a Minneapolis firefighter. It made no difference. "Check his pulse right now and tell me what it is," she insisted. But by this time she had already been warned by Thao to get up on the sidewalk, meaning that the cops disregarded her profession and expertise as they descended further into moral depravity and unyielding callousness.

And, of course, there was the game-changing witness of the valiant videographer Darnella Frazier. Brother Eric, you had three daughters, one of whom, your namesake Erica, tragically died at age twenty-seven, just three years after you were taken from her. Witnessing the deaths of loved ones exacts a high toll on our babies that is all but invisible to the outside world. And too often Black girls disappear in our culture, remaining faceless and nameless even as they offer profound inspiration to our causes and progress. Darnella was traumatized by Floyd's murder as well as by the vicious blowback she faced from folk who argued that she should have kept him from dying instead of recording his last moments on earth. If adults like Williams and Hansen couldn't halt the horizontal lynching of a Black man in broad daylight, what more might Frazier have done? With her phone's camera she has changed history and altered the narrative of Black death. If Harriet Tubman refused to give up, and Rosa Parks refused to stand up, and Fannie Lou Hamer refused to shut up, then Darnella Frazier refused to "put up" her cellphone, and in so doing inspired a revolution felt around the globe.

Brother Eric, surely Chauvin had seen the recording of your death as well, or at least had heard of it, and yet that was no deterrent to his willfully fatal actions. Prosecutors say Chauvin's knee held Floyd down for seven minutes and forty-six seconds, but a further journalistic analysis suggests it was at least nine minutes and thirty seconds. There's a moral truth here beneath the sad arithmetic that captures the hate of Black life — a numerology of nullification, a morbid mathematics of Black death. The figure 8:46 — the length of time that the original criminal complaint against Chauvin says the officer held his knee on Floyd's neck — has become more iconic and symbolic than chronometric, and will live with other tragic numbers growing out of Black grief at the hands of the police.

Floyd's death revealed the pervasive rot at the core of a system that has never treated Black folk with respect.

When the EMTs finally arrive to check George Floyd's pulse, Chauvin keeps his knee on Floyd's neck even though Floyd is completely unresponsive. Chauvin only gets off once the EMTs instruct him to let up. When the EMTs are finally about to lift Floyd's limp body, Chauvin pulls Floyd's arms, still cuffed, and helps to drag him onto the stretcher before they load him into the ambulance, which leaves the scene because of the growing crowd. The EMTs request further medical assistance from the fire department. When the truck arrives, the cops refuse to tell them where Floyd has been taken, delaying their ability to help the paramedics. Meanwhile, Floyd goes into cardiac arrest. It takes the fire engine five minutes to reach Floyd and the ambulance. He is pronounced dead at a nearby hospital about an hour after the ambulance picks him up.

This is why all the talk of abolishing and

defunding the police is crucial to reimagining their place and role in our society. Millions of white folk who couldn't have conjured in their worst nightmares the sort of brutality that Black and Brown folk encounter routinely now have seen clearly what we have been saying. Now they understand the wanton brutality that descends on Black bodies and turns them into fodder for the police force's bottomless appetite for Black subordination. Many white people saw, finally, in Chauvin's despicable act, the corrupted character of so much policing that sees itself as serving and protecting white interests. This is not about a few bad cops but about an entire system. And yet the individual effects of policing are undeniably chilling. Yes, my brother Eric, it was proof, finally, that couldn't be denied, couldn't be explained away, proof that what Black folk have been saying all along is true, that the cops often get away with murdering us even when the world is staring at them on camera.

Floyd's death amplified the cold-blooded cop killings of Breonna Taylor and Elijah McClain before him, and Rayshard Brooks shortly afterward, plunging the nation even more deeply into racial cataclysm and the determination to once and for all reckon with the deeply rooted crisis that we have failed to address.

But if the nation was poised to explode, the cops took a business-as-usual approach. Of course, Chauvin and crew claimed that Floyd resisted arrest — until restaurant surveillance footage proved that his only resistance was the refusal to get into the back of the police car. Chauvin, along with Lane, Kueng, and Thao, were fired the day after Floyd's death. The Hennepin County attorney, Mike Freeman, explained his delay in charging Chauvin by saying that "there's other evidence that does not support a criminal charge," an enraging but hardly exceptional legal ruse to stall for time. After considerable social pressure, he finally filed third-degree murder and second-degree manslaughter charges. When Minnesota governor Tim Walz appointed Minnesota attorney general Keith Ellison to take the helm of the Floyd case, Ellison quickly upgraded the charges against Chauvin to second-degree murder and charged the three other cops with aiding and abetting second-degree murder. It was a start. But it was hardly enough.

The horrid crackdown on the protesters who took to the streets in the wake of Floyd's murder — protests I shall take up in historical context in chapter 3 — also opened the eyes of many white folk to the unjust policing to which Black folk are routinely subjected. The airtight cages of resentment that trapped the police led them to rush Black and Brown — and white — bodies into custody in brutal reprisal for exercising their constitutional right to protest. No amount of what we might call "copsplaining," the police rhetoric trotted out to justify aggression against Black protesters, could effectively deconstruct the drama of denied rights and the arbitrary suspension of civil liberties unfolding before millions of white eyes.

Brother Eric, white folk finally glimpsed for themselves just a bit of what Black and Brown and Indigenous folk have been forced to see for centuries: your rights end where police paraphernalia begins. The resort to supplementing law enforcement with military forces is as clear a nod to fascist methods of social control as we have seen in many generations. The only order the cops were interested in maintaining was a social order designed to cater to "blue fragility" — the exaggerated sense of aggrievement and unjust suffering displayed by cops in light of being called to account for their racist behavior and often antidemocratic actions.

President Trump's empowered narcissism and his tragic surrender to fascist impulses have fanned the flames of racial terror, signaled the end of the right to freely protest, and suspended the liberties of law-abiding Americans. He has taken to his bully pulpit on social media to harass citizens and harangue political figures determined to restore democratic normalcy. His actions endorse an emboldened sense of domestic tyranny that is supported by the weaponized blue fragility of the cops. Both the president and the cops unleash forces that Black and Brown and Indigenous folk know like the backs of their handcuffed hands. Perhaps now this recognition among white folk — the journalists the president viciously attacks in unprincipled fashion, the citizens whose rights the cops brazenly disregard as they intimidate and arrest — will spur a profound and sustained engagement, a true racial reckoning.

Part of that reckoning means coming to grips with how we view the police. Citizens who are afraid of defunding or abolishing the police must remember that some of what turned out to be the best ideas seemed awful, radical, unworkable, disrespectful, arrogant, and, yes, revolutionary at the time

— for instance, our coming together as a country and forming a more perfect union. It is time to embrace new visions of policing in America. It is time to reimagine what it might look like if the police actually respected all citizens and helped to forge a social compact where decency could kiss order and yield relative social stability and legal harmony. It is time to imagine those responsible for public safety being committed to reducing social menace rather than reinforcing it, and to instilling respect for just laws.

It is time to reimagine the funding of social services that might reasonably redirect resources to departments and efforts that take into account mental well-being and the appropriate ways to channel humanistic energy while fostering social order. It is time to reimagine how we can reshape law enforcement so that it doesn't yield to unchecked aggression and does not undercut ethical imagination and moral concern by giving cover to racism, misogyny, and xenophobia. It is time to reimagine public safety officials as duty-bound to be policed by the society that employs them and not to view themselves as upholders of a code of conduct that subverts democracy and interrupts civil liberties. For centuries Black,

Brown, and Indigenous folk have paid too high a price in our bodies for the failures and excesses of law enforcement. Perhaps now that white bodies are at stake, now that white bodies are in play, now that white bodies are on the front lines and are tasting a bit of the concentrated chaos of policing that has destroyed our communities, genuine change is possible.

Of course, I realize that many communities of color come under fire from police brutality from the outside and crime and other destructive forces from within. There are many Black and Brown communities that crave policing that is respectful of their rights while protecting their bodies and homes. When it comes to the police, many of these communities, and the politicians who serve them, might well adapt President Clinton's phrase about affirmative action: mend, don't end, policing. Mend the hurtful gap between law enforcement and people of color so that cops become servants of the community's best interests while protecting community members from the neighborhood's worst impulses. If abolitionists can be seen as idealists who imagine a future free of the police, then many reform-minded Black folk are realists who balance the need for protection and civic decency from the cops. The abolitionists and the reformists can find middle ground as they agree on the need to shift resources, shore up community control, and institute policies of review and reform.

The big problem is that very few methods of reform have seemed to work. The harmful persistence of police brutality suggests that no amount of community policing, civilian review boards (even with extensive oversight), presidential commissions on policing, or the like has much of a chance to succeed. Police unions across the nation have accumulated enormous power and continually undermine efforts to rein in the abuse of authority by police. So it seems worth a try to approach the abolition of policing with a mind to rearrange internal relations between police departments and other agencies that address needs — especially mental health — presently gathered under the rubric of policing.

If we take into account the most exigent demands of community protection, as well as the relatively small percentage of emergency interventions that are presently called for, especially in beleaguered inner-city communities, we may be able to do two things. First, we can reconstruct the administrative infrastructure of policing so that the chain of command is shared with multiple agencies of safety and protection. Second, we can redesign the architecture of police units and disperse their duties across a number of agencies while decentralizing both their composition and their authority.

Police departments often encourage a bunker mentality of "us against the world." If they are forced to share economic and informational resources with other stakeholders in public safety, we can facilitate a transition from a sense of strict ownership reinforced by territorial domains to a cooperative enterprise driven by public service. This may also address the perilous and often harmful relationship between law enforcement and the legal system, wherein courts and prosecutors offer qualified immunity — a judicially crafted principle that protects the police from personal liability for constitutional violations like excessive force or killing citizens — to cops who misbehave and spread abuse. If qualified immunity has not so far been successfully challenged in the courts, the dismantling of police departments significantly compromises the powers that law enforcement possess. The need for qualified immunity can be significantly reduced if we make up our minds to alter the law enforcement landscape and reimagine the possibility of public safety beyond the cumbersome and constraining limits of present police departments. No matter how much argument, debate, rejiggering, and reconstruction is called for, it pales in comparison to the loss of lives occurring because of the way we do policing now.

My brother Eric, when we saw the video of George Floyd's killing, something in Black folk snapped. We realized, again, that nothing we have done has stopped the cops from taking our lives. In that moment it all came crashing down on us: Cops are the state. Cops are the white society that sees us as animals. Cops are judge and jury and may execute us at will. Thus we are all vulnerable. The shooting of Jacob Blake in the back several times in late August 2020 by a policeman in Kenosha, Wisconsin, as Blake attempted to enter his vehicle — which led to several days of protests, including the temporary shutdown of the already pandemic-delayed NBA season by striking players and the shooting and killing of two protesters by a 17-year-old white youth armed with a semi-automatic weapon — is tragic proof of this vulnerability. Fortunately he survived, although he is paralyzed from the waist down. Still, as George Floyd's death suggests, the knees of the nation have been on the necks of Black America for centuries. It took a Black man's suffering and suffocated body to pump oxygen into the body politic so that we might all breathe. But we can't stop here. Unless white folk grapple with how they have harmed the pasts and stolen the futures of Black folk, they won't be able to claim that they have participated in a true reckoning with racial oppression in America.

It always appeared a most iniquitous scheme to me — to fight ourselves for what we are daily robbing and plundering from those who have as good a right to freedom as we have.

LETTER FROM ABIGAIL ADAMS TO JOHN ADAMS ON SEPTEMBER 14, 1774

Our country was built on looting — the looting of Indigenous lands and African labor. African-Americans, in fact, have much more experience being looted than looting. . . . White mobs, often backed by the police, not only looted and burned black homes and businesses but also maimed and killed black people. Our bodies were loot. The forced extraction of our labor was loot. A system of governance that suppressed our wages, relieved us of property and excluded black people from equal schools and public accommodations is a form of looting.

— ROBIN D. G. KELLEY

# 3. WHITE THEFT

Dear Breonna Taylor,
I don't even know where to begin. I am outraged, like so many people are outraged, undoubtedly more folks than you might ever have imagined, that our democracy has failed you. Three cops barged into your apartment in Louisville, Kentucky, with a no-knock warrant and murdered you in cold blood. They didn't even identify themselves as police, and to compound the tragedy, they had the wrong person and the wrong house. Yet the police officer who killed you was neither arrested nor charged, and the lone cop who was indicted was charged only with wanton endangerment of your white neighbor. Your valiant boyfriend, Kenneth Walker, fired on the invaders, but he couldn't save you. And while the city pledged to pay your family $12 million and implement changes to prevent future deaths by cops, your killer remains free and justice

is denied.

There are so many Black women like you who have suffered similar fates but whose names we will never know. I can't imagine how horrible your boyfriend feels, how helpless he must have been in the hail of bullets that stole your life at just twenty-six. As Black men, we still want to protect the women we love. He and your family are surely inconsolable.

I think about all those young Black women like you who labor on the front lines, even during a pandemic, to make sure the rest of us are safe, keep well, and remain protected. How many young Black women are EMTs, food preparers, cashiers, mothers, babysitters, nurses, doctors, ministers, therapists, and the like, doing all they can to serve their people without much fanfare? It is tragic, too, that we have a hierarchy of victims where the names and faces of girls and women are not as brightly depicted, not as loudly proclaimed, not as well remembered and honored, as those of boys and men.

My dear sister Breonna, how many lives did you touch, even save, as you quietly went about your work? In your commitment to service, you embodied what we have taught our children from the start of our pilgrimage in this country, no matter how bleak our days or haunted our nights: to never give up. Of course, this borders on the clichéd, but the words are no less wise and worth reminding ourselves of. We are determined, as the old folk in church used to say, not to let the devil steal our joy.

My dear sister Breonna, your bright smile and gracious spirit, and the movement you have generated around the memory of your life, remind us that we were *never* what plantation owners and white supremacists claimed us to be: animals and savages, without sentiment, passion, or feelings, without regrets and aspirations, without hopes, fears, desires, and abiding love. Thomas Jefferson said of the enslaved that their "griefs are transient" and their hurts and pains "are less felt, and sooner forgotten." But the way we remember you, Breonna, shows that he was tragically wrong, that even though most of us hadn't met you before you left us, our love for you, our desire to see you get treated right, underscores just how much love can carry us forward. Your death is one of the greatest motivations for us to reckon with the long and colossal theft of our bodies, our lives, our futures, our culture, and the recognition of our worth.

Still, we have not been passive in the face

of such theft. We have resisted, and our resistance has meant life and agency in the midst of gargantuan injustices. Yet there can be no satisfactory reckoning with racial injustice that doesn't grapple with white theft of our bodies, our time, our national belonging, and so much more.

My dear sister Breonna, your life was stolen from you, just as our lives were stolen from the motherland, just as our citizenship was stolen from us even as we built this nation for no pay and with no recognition of the genius we possessed. Is it any wonder, then, that Jefferson certainly didn't have us in mind when he penned "we" in his most famous document? The "we" that dots the Declaration of Independence gathers force and definition from stating not only what Americans were but what Americans were not: *not* British, *not* "merciless savages" like the Indians, and not "domestic insurrectionists" like the Black folk. Yes, they, the royal "we," have always accused us, the disloyal "them," of rioting. They said this even as they looted and rioted and rose up against the British folk they wanted to divorce. Like them, we fought in Revolutionary times because we wanted to be free. But our bonds with the nation were continually shredded.

114

In 1857, in the *Dred Scott v. Sandford* case, the Supreme Court, under Chief Justice Roger B. Taney, declared that Black folk, enslaved or free, were not and could never be citizens of the United States of America. The Declaration of Independence may have said that "all men are created equal," but Taney contended that "it is too clear for dispute, that the enslaved African race were not intended to be included, and formed no part of the people who framed and adopted this declaration." He argued that the framers of the Constitution believed that Black folk "had no rights which the white man was bound to respect; and that the negro might justly and lawfully be reduced to slavery for his benefit. He was bought and sold and treated as an ordinary article of merchandise and traffic, whenever profit could be made by it."

My dear sister Breonna, you already know the truth of what I'm about to say. It is tiring to have to repeat it, and yet I must: America began in theft, and it has colored the nation's path ever since. That can hardly be controversial — at least it shouldn't be — and yet it is forever a thorn in the side of too many of our fellow citizens. But debates don't always get rooted in history, at least not in a history that confronts the contradictory character of the nation. Although white owners routinely had their way with enslaved women, it nearly took an act of Congress for historians to grapple with Jefferson's complicated relationship with Sally Hemings, the children they shared, and his bruising ambivalence toward slavery and Black culture.

Black folk from largely Central and West Africa were stolen from their homelands in the Atlantic slave trade. Yes, some of them were already enslaved by other Africans, though that hardly excuses what white Americans on this side of the Atlantic did in turning the tragic injustice of the slave trade into epic evil. Paradoxically, this was achieved when the entire enterprise got religion and its advocates preached that God rescued the savages from heathenism on the dark continent and brought them to salvation through slavery in North America. But no amount of evangelical fervor for the souls of the enslaved could mask the fact that Black flesh was stolen — in truth, looted — from our beleaguered motherland.

The theft of body and breath continued on the voyage to the New World, where millions were victims of spatial violence, crammed like sardines into ships, and often lost at sea in the perilous Middle Passage.

The Western white world continually returned to the scene of the crime to heist more bodies and hoist them onto vessels that spread them throughout the Western Hemisphere. But the theft and looting did not end once Black folk got to North America. For nearly three hundred years the routine theft of Black limb and labor stole from Black culture our futures and freedoms and reimagined us as the tools of white leisure and greed. White folk stole from us the very measure of time and space that they sought our bodies to supplement. They tirelessly exploited the ingenuity they swore we sorely lacked.

In slavery, Black folk fought back as much as they could, stealing back their bodies in what might be termed the political economy of night. While slave rebellions garnered the most press, the enslaved found myriad creative ways to steal back their time. They faked sickness, broke tools, spoiled crops, and injured animals. They also slowed down work and stretched out the day, performing as little labor as possible while sneaking in naps when the overseer was distracted. But it was at night that they were revived by traveling many miles to attend dances, hunt, fish, worship, and steal food. Slave masters bitterly noted that while their young men may have been sluggish during the day, they came alive at night when it was time to visit their wives and girlfriends. White folk called the night the "Nigger day-time." As white folk retreated with their families into their homes, Black folk, especially boys and young men, floated and darted about. The separation of night and day was more than a chronological measure; it divided the tyranny of the overseer's whip and the master's tightfisted control from the enslaved's episodic emancipation in the dark. This was one way they stole back a measure of autonomy, exercised agency, and resisted complete submission to slavery.

The enslaved cultivated a sense of entitlement to fight off the white perception that they were shiftless and unworthy beings. They used the political economy of night to support their belief that they deserved the luxuries and leisure that their hard work afforded lazy owners. Imagination became a tool of self-defense. But imagination was both conceptual and strategic: it was both an idea the enslaved used to craft self-images that governed their conduct and a means to bolster their beliefs and achieve their aspirations. The enslaved imagination was fed as they watched in envy the leisure of white men who devoured chicken, eggs, beef, and pork washed down by plentiful beverages. As their eyes widened their minds expanded. At night the enslaved were on the hunt to fulfill their imaginations and fill their bellies.

If the enslaved had already taken up residence in the white imagination, working overtime as figures of desire and repulsion, pursuit and resentment, worry and fear, then white folk occupied the Black imagination and fueled Black desire too. In order for the enslaved to achieve their goals, and to emulate white society, they resorted to theft. The Black imagination offered the enslaved space to rehearse — centuries in advance — forms of equality their descendants might later enjoy. The political economy of night temporarily righted the scales of justice, allowing Black folk to claw at the outer edges of freedom and, if not financial parity, at least culinary equity. Beyond the symbolic value of eating like the master, it permitted Black folk to tap into the cultural dimensions of equality and freedom beyond the economic realm.

Thus, when the enslaved sought pigs and sheep and finer cuts of meat in emulating white folk, their desires were not merely in pursuit of capitalist conveniences but were infused with political overtones and symbolic meanings. The political economy of night helped the enslaved to organize and execute plans to run away to find freedom, or to establish communities of maroons on the borderlands of plantations or in the vaster, wilder hinterlands, renegade societies that were outside the crushing boundaries of slavery. Often these experiments in fugitive democracy ended in men, women, and children dying, but they preferred to perish in the wilderness rather than face enslavement and violent punishment should they return to the plantation. Indeed, it was a brutal beating that had driven many of them into the woods with their shackles still attached, marking them clearly as recent runaways. Some of them never recovered from their severe punishment and died in their fetters. Others made the impossible decision to return because they felt they had no choice. It was devastating to have to submit once again to white control and the pitiless exercise of near-total power. But whatever the path, their valiant efforts to resist slavery were aided through routine theft.

Some of the maroons returned to the plantation at night to steal hogs and chickens. When they braved the wild, the maroons lived by their wits and skill, trapping, snaring, shooting, and fishing. They took advantage of their proximity to their former plantations and caught and killed cattle and hogs that belonged to the white farmers but which half lived in the wild. It wasn't just the maroons who stole, but poor whites too, runaways, and of course the enslaved.

The enslaved had no moral regrets about getting from farms and plantations what was called in the vernacular "stold stuff" to feed themselves. They justified their theft with sophisticated appraisals of the value of their labor. One slave even cleverly reasoned that since he was property, and the animals he stole from his master were as well, it made sense that one facet of his property benefit the other. When some masters shorted their slaves of adequate food, some of the enslaved would lead a pig or sheep a few miles into the woods to kill it and feed those who were being starved, becoming heroes in their quarters.

Despite the cleverness and creativity that marked their political economy of night, the enslaved constantly ran up against the tyrannical force of ruthless owners, planters, and overseers. These white powers sought to extract even more work from the slaves so that they could wear them out and discourage their nighttime activities. When the suspicion of rebellion was in the air, things got even more brutal. In the early 1700s the owners and overseers called on slave patrols, militia, and other police forces to cruelly enforce laws, restrictions, and punishment. The slave patrols, which largely though not exclusively drew from the ranks of the poor, took nearly sadistic delight in lashing the flesh of the enslaved, and at times torturing, terrorizing, or even killing them.

To steal was a way for the stolen to take back what had been taken from them. The political economy of night saw the enslaved deprive their owners of their labor, of their will, of their energy, in small acts of resistance and bigger acts of defiance or outright subversion. The enslaved also physically fought back throughout slavery. They took what was meant for labor in the daytime and transformed those items into weapons of resistance, using boosted pistols, rifles, scythes, corn cutters, and other farm tools. The scythes that were fitted with a short, straight handle were the weapon of choice against the bloodhounds that were ceaselessly unleashed on Black folk. When that didn't work, they used "stagger pizen," poison made of a noxious plant indigenous to the southern swamp that made animals stagger as if they were intoxicated until they drew their last breaths.

Black folk who escaped to freedom, or who were already free outside the South, fought back through vigilance committees to protect runaways. They took more aggressive measures by forming Black militias like the Attucks Guards in New York and Cincinnati. The escape of the enslaved provoked new forms of Black militancy in states where slavery had been officially outlawed. Before the 1850s, free Black folk diligently created networks to harbor fugitives and to defend them against marauding slave catchers. Free Blacks also built settlements, guarded thoroughfares, and inspected docks in the effort to rescue other free Blacks who were being kidnapped.

The Christiana Riot in Pennsylvania is one dramatic example of Black self-defense. The Fugitive Slave Act passed by Congress in 1850 mandated the return of all escaped slaves to their southern owners. The next year Maryland slaveholder Edward Gorsuch and his son and some of their neighbors, along with federal officials and two Philadelphia police officers, headed to Lancaster, Pennsylvania, in the late summer to retrieve four older male runaways, Noah Buley, Nelson Ford, George Hammond, and

Joshua Hammond. Gorsuch believed that because he was a relatively decent owner, freeing the enslaved at the age of twenty-eight and then afterward offering them compensation for seasonal work, they would return. The Philadelphia police officers hired by Gorsuch to make the arrest turned back when they realized that the local Black community had been warned that they were coming. The Gorsuch party was brought up short at the home of resistance leader William Parker, himself an escaped slave, by between 75 and 150 Black men and women and white abolitionists brandishing a variety of weapons. Gorsuch was killed in the fracas; his son was mortally wounded. The rest of the group was routed.

After the Civil War, law enforcement took on half of the slave patrol's tasks, as they obsessed over suspicious Black folk, haunted the nighttime social gatherings of Black people, and tracked down lawbreakers, while the other half of the slave patrol's mission, its most violent and terrorizing aspects, was taken up by white vigilante groups like the Ku Klux Klan. From Reconstruction well into the twentieth century, law enforcement and racial terrorists (who were sometimes drawn from the ranks of the police) fed from the same trough. Although police were not exact replicas of the slave patrols, they nevertheless drew inspiration and encouragement plus methods and approaches from their heartless predecessors. In tandem with white vigilantism, law enforcement has tried to put down Black revolution, contain Black rebellion, and use the law to justify aggressive action against Black protest in the streets.

In many ways, the slave patrols, and later law enforcement, were the instruments of the state used to protect the theft of Black life and of the rights and privileges of full citizenship. The police not only brutalized Black bodies but dented the armor of social equality and civil rights by threatening the physical safety, civic well-being, and politi cal progress of Black culture. If the state stole, the police protected its theft and discouraged rebellion against its unjust practices. There is no greater sign of such efforts at ruthless containment as when the police flood the streets to meet and turn back Black bodies on the march for justice.

My dear sister Breonna, much like what tragically happened to you when you were mercilessly gunned down, what is happening now in our nation's streets seems like a crude translation of Thomas Hobbes's *bel-*

*lum omnium contra omnes,* the war of all against all. But a far more specific battle is playing out. In many ways it is the continuation of the historical battles we have waged to steal back our bodies and time and rights and wealth and culture.

But that battle may also be pictured as a struggle between the Black "next" and the white "again," competing approaches to democracy that register our buoyant hopes and mark our turbulent fears. Perhaps no word better sums up Black life — its noble political aspirations, its relentless cultural creativity, its quest for survival — than "next." Black imagination fuels immortal moves onstage, in the athletic arena, and on pages and screens of every sort. Black folk are rarely satisfied with whatever artistic expression is at hand, or with whatever state of political affairs is given. This dissatisfaction sparks the quest for the next cultural creation and the next phase of racial advance. Field hollers gave way to spirituals, which birthed the blues, which unfurled in jazz, which propelled rhythm and blues, which enflamed soul music and ignited rock and roll, which radiated in funk, which in turn unleashed hip hop. Slave rebellions inspired abolition and war, echoing later in freedom struggles against southern apartheid, which led to civil rights struggles to vote and travel and live as we pleased.

Each moment of Black creation is met with white theft; each gesture of Black advance is dogged by retaliation. Each Black "next" is opposed by a white "again." Of course, Black folk have turned even white appropriation and opposition to our advantage as inspiration for the next artistic style or as a prod to the next form of political resistance. Appropriation is a muted form of the original theft of Black bodies; it only seems like a more genial form of stealing. The death of rock and roll pioneer Little Richard compelled us to reconsider his legacy and helped restore luster to a figure who was not always credited as the primary architect of the genre, underscoring how the origin story of Black genius can be obscured, even erased, with the substitution of white talent.

Erasure, substitution, and reinvention happen time and again. The envy of Blackness is as constant as the resentment of Black artistic expression; they lead to the theft of Black cultural forms, brazenly and unapologetically ripping off Black culture and diluting it to aesthetic death, then remaking and repackaging it. Black culture finds a way to reinvent itself, to release new creative energy, to go on to the next thing, invent the next style after an original Black sound has been stolen, bought, bowdlerized, censored, emended, edited, redacted, reformed, and appropriated — glimpsed in the way Black jazz musicians generated bebop from the streets to contest the white takeover of swing music on the bandstand.

In the social and political order, the Black "next" insists on the new, the hopeful, the transformative, often against any possibility of its realization. The white "again" bitterly clings to the past. If Black politics and the culture of "next" have often expressed the desire to make history anew, then the white world of the stubborn "again" holds fast to a highly selective version of the past. The white "again" cloaks its centuries-long will to control Black bodies in talk of tradition and conserving values. The white "again" seeks ways to deny Black progress.

The Black "next" is ferociously persistent despite the violent resistance it confronts. When Black folk sought to get to the next level of upward mobility through education, white dominance tried again and again to limit Black learning to schools with inadequate resources. Black folk fought back and got a victory with the 1954 *Brown v. Board of Education* decision, even as the present sweep of resegregated schools proves the white "again" is dishonorably consistent. When Black folk attempted to integrate buses in Montgomery, Alabama, in 1955, the Black "next" faced a moody and malicious white "again" that sought to keep Black folk in their place at the back of the bus. But the Supreme Court ruled in Blacks' favor, and, in this climate, white folk lynched Willie Edwards, a Black man accused of flirting with a white woman, and they fired on the house of the newly minted young leader Martin Luther King Jr. Black folk fought to reach the next rung on the social and political ladder by eating at lunch counters, staying in public accommodations, voting in the South, and gaining fair housing; the white "again" tried to assert its veto power with crushing rules that reinforced Black dislocation in civil society and traced its way across the map via steering, redlining, and blockbusting.

If every defiant Black "next" has been met with a resentful white "again," if every Black effort to move, mobilize, shake off white obstruction, and advance to the next stage, the next arena, and the next platform has struck fear in the heart of white America, it has also revealed how Black folk, the denied inheritors of the American prosperity they made possible, have more faithfully fulfilled the moral ambitions, political intentions, and social aspirations of democracy than many of their white peers. The Black "next" has always revealed a deep belief in the nation, a love that is persistent, unshakable, and, yes, necessarily tough. Black rage is hope turned inside out. Unlike those who sulked into secession, Black folk stayed to fight against the dying of the democratic light. Against nearly every shred of evidence and contrary to our collective intuition, there lingers a profound hope and a deep love.

The white "again" is a refusal to let true democracy take hold. Those who actually believe in this country are those who, out of utter frustration, civic humiliation, or racial solidarity, have taken to the streets to protest. Those whose belief in America is shaky are the ones opposing Black citizens who simply want to enjoy the same rights they do, who want the same benefit of the doubt offered to them. If earlier generations of white folk denied Black folk opportunities and stole their land and limbs, too many in the present age simply update their efforts and attempt, again, to hold Black folk back. While many of us manage to progress from social pariah to social staple in all manner of cultural and professional endeavors, far more of us are denied the right to flourish, or even to exist. Yet those of us who remain persist. "Next" is progress; "again" is stasis. There can be no real reckoning with our racial crisis if we don't fully attend to the push and pull of the Black "next" and the white "again." That is the defining fight, not only of Black folk but of the nation.

My dear sister Breonna, the conflict between "next" and "again" plays out on the battlefield of ideas too. The 1619 Project, led by *New York Times* writer Nikole Hannah-Jones, argued that the legacy of slavery is central to the nation's founding and identity, and may indeed have furnished the thirteen colonies a rationale for taking up arms. That was a rare instance where the Black "next" claimed a louder and more official voice than the white "again." But, predictably, the white "again" — with its arthritic defense of the status quo — rose up in what might be termed a white verbal riot. Distinguished white historians Sean Wilentz, James McPherson, Gordon Wood, Victoria Bynum, and James Oakes criticized Jones and the 1619 Project, claiming in a letter to the *Times* that the project promoted "a displacement of historical understanding by ideology." Arkansas senator Tom Cotton introduced legislation to deny federal funds to teach the 1619 Project in the nation's public schools. Cotton may not be the most reliable guide to the nation's complicated racial history. On the one hand, he is critical of the 1619 Project for arguing that the colonies chose the Revolutionary War in part to protect slavery. On the other hand, Cotton admits that the Founding Fathers viewed the enslavement of millions of Black souls as "the necessary evil upon which the union was built."

Of course, there have been white riots in which Black lives were lost and Black property burned to the ground. But there are quieter white riots that burn down Black progress in government, in academe, in think tanks, in corporate America, and in the media. Black ideas are viewed as bankrupt and Black arguments are seen as rooted in wishful thinking and racial vengeance against the white establishment. A country that gushes as it stands beneath an endless avalanche of history books about every imaginable aspect of the nation's trek from fledgling colonial upstart to imperial superpower grows grim and mum, with notable exceptions, when it comes to soaking in historical cascades of the slave past.

Histories that spring from the white "again" have been forced to address race and slavery but don't dig nearly as deep as those histories steeped in or inspired by the Black "next." The Black "next" seems so radical, so antithetical to what we know, because it stands against what was silenced and hidden. It's not that the Black "next" is new; it's that it is newly revealed, uncovered, exposed. To consider the idea that keeping folk enslaved was at least on the minds of the architects of the American Revolution as they combated British tyranny is sacrilege to those who seek to maintain the status quo — those who seek to put forth a more "innocent" and "pure" version of the past, again and again.

The sort of history that seeks to cast the past as innocent and pure is constantly at war with the sort of mature and complicated history that will help us reckon with race in a satisfying fashion. That struggle has no clearer expression than on the battlefield of memory and mythology as protesters take aim at Confederate statues, Confederate flags, and other monuments to global empire and racism. The moral and political vision of the Confederacy has been clear for decades to even the slightly curious. Its denizens were traitors to America; its hearty defense of slavery fed its resentment of Black progress; it was willing to fight to the death to defend the proposition that white theft of Black bodies was their God-given right. Those who embrace the Confederacy can no more avoid embracing those ideas than a Christian can avoid embracing Jesus.

The proud and rabid celebration of the Confederacy is the ultimate white "again" pitted against the most energetic Black "next." The statues of Confederate heroes have for far too long littered the landscape of a country that the Confederacy's adherents believed should not exist. Those symbols of the Confederacy are supported by citizens who despise the anti-Americanism they think fuels principled Black protests against injustice even as they fly the flag of a traitorous confederation of bigots. Neither can we defend the avid support of the Confederacy as a matter of heritage when it is clear that the hate of Black folk is the premise of its very existence. It is a good thing for those statues and flags to be removed, and it would even be better (though unlikely) to replace them with statues of figures who fought and died to make America a better place for all of its citizens.

■ ■ ■

Dear Breonna, if Black folk have battled over the history of ideas in the effort to leverage our Black "next" against the white "again," we have sought as well to draw on a resonant Black past to drive progress in the present. It is an apt reminder, too, that any effort to reckon with race must grapple with the habits of Black survival and the historical context for Black flourishing. In this manner, such Black efforts affirm William Faulkner's wisdom: "The past is never dead. It's not even past." Black folk seek to extend the moral trajectory of the Black "next" into contemporary struggle. Despite stubborn obstacles to Black progress, Black bodies continue to flourish in the political economy of night. As was true in slavery, much of the daytime belongs to interactions with white bosses or colleagues. But after work there is a Black exodus away from white spaces. Black folk use this "Black time" to sustain rituals of cultural cohesion, deepen racial ties, enhance collective identity, and nurture Black survival. The political economy of night is also used to forge stronger civic ties to political organizations and social movements as Black folk together envision a better future. Yes, there are Black gatherings aimed at figuring out how to gain a greater share of the American prosperity that Black labor has made possible. And there is even Black folks' insistence on integrating and invading white space and time to bring the priorities of the political economy of the night to vibrant expression in the day.

The political economy of the night has fostered several dimensions of Black life that flourished at night during slavery: dances, or, more broadly, entertainment; hunting and fishing, or the pursuit of sport; worship; advocacy of armed self-defense; and the planning of protest and social rebellion.

Black entertainment associated with the night, from juke joints to concert halls, from after-hours clubs to swanky nightspots, afforded Black entertainers the opportunity to inspire the masses with song and dance, provided a crucial social outlet, and offered spaces of Black revelry that permitted talented figures to hone their talents. Long before the rise of the Internet and social media, the chitlin circuit gave Black folk a taste of Black genius up close in small joints and boutique Black clubs across America, as well as in larger venues like Detroit's Fox Theater, Chicago's Regal Theater, and

Harlem's Apollo Theater. The political economy of night transformed the rites and ecstasies of Black cultural performances into sustaining expressions that offered unqualified endorsement of Black aesthetics, the enthusiastic validation of Black styles of speech, dress, and relaxation, and the lively legitimization of Black expressions of social intimacy, amusement, and leisure. Black audiences often rendered harsh judgment, pushing Black entertainers to refine their performance, even as they gave the Black collective say-so over the best examples of Black excellence. Before Louis Armstrong, Duke Ellington, Billie Holiday, Dinah Washington, Ella Fitzgerald, Sarah Vaughn, Little Richard, Chuck Berry, Ray Charles, Aretha Franklin, and countless other Black artists took the white world by storm, they first had to please a far harder audience: the Black folk who gave the political economy of night a vibrant voice and vital vision. Their relatively unique position in the white world at that time gave Black entertainers the motivation to speak out against racial oppression in America. Before there were outspoken artists in our day like Alicia Keys and John Legend, there were courageous critics of racism like artists Hazel Scott and Sam Cooke.

Black sport, too, grew out of the political economy of night, as Black athletes sought outlets to develop their skills and broaden their base of support. When they were denied participation in white amateur sports leagues, amateur Black athletes sharpened their skills in Black circles, if not always at night. As professional leagues developed, they often barred Black athletes, and Blacks eventually formed their own leagues, whether amateur, semipro, or professional, and they were often sponsored by athletic clubs, colored YMCAs, and churches. The sight of men and women displaying athletic achievement in Black circles inspired Black folk in the stands or arenas. The sight of those fans in turn fueled the passion of athletes, just as it had with entertainers, to represent Black political interests and to speak out for the masses of Black folk and their quest for social justice. LeBron James and Maya Moore are brilliant athletes who carry a bright torch for social justice in our day, as Jackie Robinson and Althea Gibson held high the banner of social justice in an earlier epoch.

Black worship was central to the political economy of night. Even as the major religious services of the Black Christian church occurred on Sundays, the Black church also frequently met during the week at night. In slavery, the "invisible institution" secretly convened in "hush harbors" where Black folk gathered to praise their God and pray for peaceful survival amid the storms of suffering. At other times, they preached deliverance from their political predicament. Increasingly, the church that gathered at night accommodated more aggressive visions of exodus. It is no coincidence that Gabriel Prosser, Nat Turner, and Denmark Vesey, leaders of three of the most storied slave revolts, were all deeply religious men. And the great emancipator Harriet Tubman was a profoundly religious woman. Well after slavery Black folk met in their religious institutions to plan social resistance to racial oppression. Many Black preachers became leaders of Black freedom struggles, from abolitionist and radical minister Henry Highland Garnet in the 1800s to Martin Luther King Jr. in the twentieth century. The success of the Montgomery bus boycott depended on many nighttime meetings where leaders like Jo Ann Robinson, Rosa Parks, Ralph Abernathy, and King plotted strategy and where the folk gathered to pray, praise, and promote protest. Pauli Murray and C. L. Franklin, Aretha's father, were activist clergy in the sixties and seventies, and Al Sharpton and Vashti McKenzie wear the mantle today.

Just as free Blacks and the enslaved took up their own defense, contemporary movements of self-defense have arisen too. Black folk drew on the ranks of men returning from military service to form armed groups to defend Black communities in the early twentieth century. Scores of Black folk throughout the South organized informally to protect themselves and their property against vengeful and violent white mobs in the first half of the twentieth century. They were inspired by figures like the pioneering Black journalist and anti-lynching activist Ida B. Wells-Barnett, who in the late 1800s argued that Black folk should aggressively defend themselves. She contended that a "Winchester rifle should have a place of honor in every Black home, and it should be used for that protection which the law refuses to give." Groups of armed Black men took up the call for self-defense during racial strife in places like Wilmington, North Carolina, in 1898, in Evansville, Indiana, in 1903, in Atlanta in 1906, and in Springfield, Illinois, in 1908. Black self-defense was sometimes planned, as when Black military veterans of the 8th Regiment donned their uniforms and took up arms to prevent mob violence during a race riot in Chicago in 1919, and at other times it was spontaneous, occurring when Black men, for instance, went to work, got attacked, and fought back.

Throughout the fifties, sixties, and seventies, strands of Black social resistance advocated self-defense. Among the most famous self-defense groups were the Deacons for Defense and Justice, founded in Louisiana in 1964; even earlier, there were self-defense activities in North Carolina, outlined in the groundbreaking book *Negroes with Guns,* authored by civil rights activist Robert F. Williams. During the Black Lives Matter movement in 2020 a new pro-gun Black self-defense militia, the Not F——king Around Coalition (NFAC), emerged. Its members, decked out in military fatigues and sporting semiautomatic weapons, agitated many white folk while drawing great acclaim in some Black circles because of their attendance at protests like one that urged the arrest of the officers who killed you, dear sister Breonna, in Louisville, Kentucky, where white militia had appeared in threatening formation.

Of course, across the decades the political economy of night has been used by Black freedom fighters to fill the air with ringing protests against injustice. The present stage of sustained protests against racial injustice, inspired by your death, dear sister Breonna, and those of Ahmaud Arbery and George Floyd, has tapped into the long tradition of radical resistance that has been refreshingly multiracial and intergenerational. The revolutionary cries of Black Lives Matter rest upon a simple yet poignant foundation: that Black lives, which haven't mattered, should matter, and that we must reform the criminal justice system, greatly change if not abolish the police, and grapple with systemic racism. Part of the lethal legacy of slavery and white supremacy is the impoverishment of vast reaches of Black America. Black Lives Matter and most other Black freedom movements have attempted to address the vicious consequences of slavery's legacy in Black life: the theft of Black land, social opportunity, and social mobility; the prison industrial complex; inequities in education, employment, and housing. All these have left many Black folk permanently poor, vulnerable to disease, socially dislocated, and resorting to crime, especially stealing food to feed families or engaging in other illegal activities to support kin.

The political economy of night has often in such cases been transformed into the underground political economy. It is here that Black folk have begged, borrowed, bartered, fenced, and stolen their way to a meager existence amidst the colossal and unacknowledged theft of their livelihoods over the centuries. From drug dealers, hustlers, thieves, and pimps to those trying to provide a hedge against financial insecurity by painting houses, shoveling snow, or mowing lawns, Black folk in the informal economy — some of them poor and working-class — do whatever is necessary to make ends meet. While public moralists and social critics weigh in on the self-destructive character of the underground political economy, they offer little insight about the devastating impact of anti-Black social policies and destructive racial politics on the desperately poor. And while critics draw direct lines between such behavior in the underground economy and the looting and theft that occasionally occur amidst social protest, they refuse to draw lines of cause and effect between the white theft of Black futures, freedoms, and financial stability over the centuries and the vulnerable economic and social position of the Black permanently poor today. Neither do they propose reparations as a moral and economic redress for the systematic looting of Black culture over the last four hundred years.

The powerful rise of the Black "next" in contemporary Black protest as we reckon with systemic racism has been met by the reactionary forces of the white "again," notably President Trump, who has commandeered military forces to descend on American cities in a profane violation of civic virtue and the rights of citizens to assemble and argue on their feet for the social good. This president has set a political precedent that not even our most acidly conservative leaders have dared to establish. The trumping up of false allegations against protesters — that they are troublemaking anarchists, that they hate America, that they are the reason racial justice continues to be thwarted — is part of the ratcheting up of racial bigotry. It is a cynical summons of the biting words of white nationalism from a deep cesspool of racial intolerance — a gesture that, in concert with the president's other politically destructive moves, has the nation teetering on the edge of the neo-fascist abyss. The white "again" has rarely possessed a voice that echoes disdain for racial justice as loudly as Trump's.

The white "again" thwarts Black progress by extending the bitter past. In too many ways, the failure to support the Black "next" over the white "again" spills over in the anger that occasionally flares up in the streets. As for the rare folk who have destroyed property, there is often the rebuttal: it makes no sense to destroy your own neighborhood. But what does a neighborhood mean if a cop can come onto your street and — in your case, dear sister Breonna — into your home and kill you? If you don't own your own body, what, in the end, do you really own? Those flames seem unwarranted to many white brothers and sisters. But when they decry Black self-destruction, they often ignore the systemic white destruction of Black life and neighborhoods.

And those contrasting Black self-destruction with the quest for fair play and righteous conduct rarely stop to consider that when Black folk politely ask for justice, make calm arguments, try to reason with the powers that be, they are rarely heard. When former professional quarterback Colin Kaepernick, as part of the Black "next," took a knee on the gridiron to highlight police brutality, the white "again" portrayed him as if he had attempted to send society to its death. They went so far as to banish him from the National Football

League. Then, too, the history of white theft, of white looting, of white stealing of Black time and space, of Black limbs and lives, of the white canvassing of Black cultures for booty and benefit, is forever masked beneath either a tart denial of white complicity in social evil or a doubling down on the belief that the white "again" is the only way to save the country from the Black "next."

When Martin Luther King Jr. gave speeches, he was often applauded, with little action following, but when his fight against injustice provoked police forces to violently train their dogs and water hoses on Black flesh, civil rights legislation was passed. Some critics contend that contemporary protests fuel violence and destroy property, unlike sixties' protests led by King and other activists when mostly Black bodies were at risk. Yet our bodies are still at risk as Black folk clash with cops in uprisings and on countless street corners. For some Black folk it is better to risk our lives fighting for justice than to die with the knees of cops, and therefore white society, forever fixed on our necks. This may be seen as history coming full circle: the looted and stolen now in a far tamer and less consequential fashion loot and steal. Folk often quote Martin

Luther King Jr. when he spoke out against riots. But he was quick to add that he would never speak out against rioters without also speaking out against "the greatest purveyor of violence," the American government. Since cops are still on the government payroll, King's statement rings true. So does his statement that the "white man['s] . . . police make a mockery of law."

But it was white America that rejected King's vision of nonviolence — not Black folk. America wouldn't listen to what non-violent Black folk said, so now they are speaking differently — not violently, but far more aggressively. The shame of contemporary riots, uprisings, and rebellions does not belong to those in the streets; the shame is that it took even a little destruction of property for them to be heard. That's a criticism of the arbiters of "again," not the advocates of "next." Our unflappable "next" against the nation's Herculean "again" is the titanic fight that may yet determine our nation's future.

Dear sister Breonna, in your name, and in the name of so many other souls laid low by injustice and hate — such as Daniel Prude, a Rochester, N.Y., man who had a psychotic episode and had a hood placed on his head and was held down by police as they arrested him, only to die a week later in the hospital — we must not permit the despair of the white "again" to drain the hope of the Black "next." The Black "next" has bravely combatted the cynical lies of white supremacy and the stubborn resistance of the white "next."

But there is one way that we have surrendered to a feint, a mirage, a truculent deceit. While Black folk have stolen back our time, our bodies, and our culture as much as we can from the white "again," as we reckon with massive inequalities we must resist the temptation to steal an idea, that of cancel culture, that promises justice but delivers chaos.

A child cannot, thank Heaven, know how vast and how merciless is the nature of power, with what unbelievable cruelty people treat each other.

— JAMES BALDWIN

# 4. SEEING RED

Dear Hadiya Pendleton,
Even though I didn't have the honor of meeting you, I feel a special bond with you, as if you were a young lady I'd have seen in church when I was preaching or would have chatted with at one of the high schools where I frequently speak. It would have made me happy to listen to your plans or offer you a word of encouragement to pursue your dreams. Even though I didn't know you, it hurts when I think of how your life was snatched by a cruel twist of fate. Your future looked so promising. I cannot even imagine the suffering of your parents, who have to live every day with the thought that you were cut down before you were able to fly into your destiny.

Precious Hadiya, of course I feel connected to you too because you were from Chicago and I twice lived and taught in the "Chi." President Obama spoke of you at his

2013 State of the Union address, which your parents attended as his guests, two weeks after you lost your life a mile from his Chicago home. "She loved Fig Newtons and lip gloss," he said of you. "She was a majorette. She was so good to her friends they all thought they were her best friend." I wept as the globe's most powerful man eulogized a gifted and beautiful Black girl.

Unlike most of the other martyrs I've addressed, your death at just fifteen didn't come at the hands of a cop or a vigilante. You died when a young Black man mistook your group of friends for a rival gang and shot you in the back. I have written and spoken time and again against the notion of "Black-on-Black crime." The more accurate and insightful way to speak about such deaths, the way to avoid scapegoating communities of color, is to talk of neighbor-on-neighbor carnage. The fact is that people usually kill where they live: the vast majority of Black folk who are killed are indeed killed by other Black folk, and the same holds true for white folk.

Of course, poverty, hopelessness, and lack of opportunity breed desperation, mayhem, and bloodbaths. It's more than a shame that a city like Chicago is caught between vicious cycles of police brutality and waves of

destruction that batter neighbor after neighbor, community after community. And too
many folks who should know and care better display a harsh disregard for Black youth
that only makes an already untenable situation worse. Folk in conservative media and
think tanks are always saying that Black folk
get riled up by police killings but stay silent
when Black death comes at the hands of
one of our own.

It's a strange way to think of these things.
And it never escapes me that the same
media speaking of "one of our own" gets
incensed when that language is used to suggest Black unity. Then it's "Why can't you
guys be individuals and not part of a
group?" But when it's convenient for their
politics, then we are thrown into the same
pot as one indistinguishable mess. Plus, it's
not true that Black folk don't care unless
the person doing the killing is blue. I have
participated in many marches in favor of
greater safety in our neighborhoods. Your
death hurts. But responsibility goes beyond
the young Black man who pulled the trigger
and the one who drove the getaway car.
Their lives are lost too, sacrificed to a
criminal justice system that will warehouse
them but hardly rehabilitate them.

Precious Hadiya, sometimes I fantasize

that it will all go away, that it will just stop. But the tragedy is that there are still too many Hadiyas and too many young Black men who are killing them, and too much poverty and grief and drugs and gangs and hopelessness and horror and terror and shrinking opportunities and rising racism. It's an ache that won't go away.

Some people, understandably upset, understandably enraged, just want to get rid of young men like the ones involved in your murder. I understand the anger, the heartbreak, and the fear, the fear that it won't ever stop unless we put an end to it somehow, the fear that it won't disappear unless we make it disappear, or at least make the folk who commit the carnage disappear. Wipe them out. Send them away. For good. I get that in my gut and my heart. You should be here, precious Hadiya. You should be alive.

When I was a teen, my pastor gave a sermon that drew from the scripture about the disconsolate prophet Elijah in 1 Kings 19:4: "But he himself went a day's journey into the wilderness, and came and sat down under a juniper tree: and he requested for himself that he might die; and said, It is enough; now, O LORD, take away my life; for I am not better than my fathers." The pastor titled his sermon "Cancel Tomorrow," suggesting the prophet wanted God to cancel his tomorrows and let him die. Many of us want to cancel the tomorrows of people who have canceled other people's tomorrows.

But it is never that simple, precious Hadiya. To put to death those who killed you is not really to address the circumstances that led to such slaughter, such destruction, such grief and suffering. It would be vengeance, for sure, but I'm not so certain about justice. The pain will continue because the actions won't stop. And if there is any role for redemption, rehabilitation, or restoration of any sort, then it seems a humane society should hold out the possibility that something might change. Full accountability? Yes, of course. Restorative justice? That too.

Precious Hadiya, in one measure it's a big relief that the issue I want to address here is not nearly as serious and profound as your death. I broach your killing here because I want to honor your memory and honor the pain that surrounds your loss. But I also want to acknowledge that there are different ways to address such violence, different visions of what it means and how we change it. And that is true for our reckoning generally with the racial crisis in this country.

There is a great deal of righteous anger about our failure to achieve racial justice. Centuries of hurt and pain have built up, and now that the racial dam has burst there is a war of ideas about race, about how we see the past, the present, and our future, that is just as vigorous as our discussions about death in the streets. The war of ideas and the deaths, though of a substantially different order of magnitude, are nevertheless linked: both grow out of hopelessness and anger. In our reckoning, we need to keep one in mind as we ponder the other — we must keep our minds on the tragic consequences that you suffered, precious Hadiya, while we keep our eyes on the best route to justice. I know that it is tempting to go the way of least resistance and quickest resolution. But some forms of apparent justice seem to me little more than a perilous and fascist surrender to the sort of vengeance that can never satisfy the moral demands for positive change.

About a month after George Floyd's death, and in the thick of the largest protests for social justice the nation has ever seen, I got an invitation to sign a letter that argued for greater racial and gender justice in the classroom, the newsroom, and the arts, and for greater tolerance of political differences and open debate. So far so good, since I'm always in favor of more justice and more free-flowing debate. Plus, a partial list of people signing the letter included folk I admire, like poet Reginald Dwayne Betts, philosopher Drucilla Cornell, historian Nell Irvin Painter, and, I later found out, linguist and social critic Noam Chomsky. When I read the letter, however, I wasn't nearly as enthusiastic.

Mind you, I agreed with a fair bit of what was presented, especially that we cannot adopt dogma over intellectual engagement. Still, I advised the colleague who had sent it to me to hold off on publishing the letter. Only the first sentence took note of our racial crisis, and it just barely acknowledged the dreadful consequences that most Black folk were facing. With its greater focus on free expression, it seemed more than a tad indulgent and, quite frankly, narcissistic. I told him that it would inevitably be seen as a reactionary gesture at precisely the time when Black folk were finally gaining some traction in getting issues of racism on the national agenda in a way not seen since the sixties. Yes, perhaps the signers opposed virulent bigotry and systemic racism, but the point of things now, of course, is that white folk have to reexamine their institutions and practices and make plain their allegiances. Otherwise the letter, which was later revealed as the brainchild of Black expat writer Thomas Chatterton Williams, would appear absurdly tone deaf.

I argued that releasing the letter now — even with a smattering of Black voices from across the ideological spectrum — would only reinforce the perception of a smug and self-interested intelligentsia worrying about how this would all affect the mostly white writers. Precious Hadiya, I said that their posture recalled the liberal white clergy cautioning Martin Luther King Jr. in a public statement about the harmful effect on the social order of too-quick and too-radical demands for social change. In response, King, embroiled in the effort to integrate a violent American city, penned the glorious "Letter from Birmingham Jail." I told my colleague that the letter signers were setting themselves up as the white clergy, not Martin Luther King, which wasn't a good thing.

As we reckon with racial change in the culture, there are many avenues to challenge the powers that be. One approach seems to be a reversal of the status quo but really is no reversal at all. Instead it is the troubling reappearance of an idea and behavior that were first broadcast in Black culture but which have deep and harmful roots in white society. In brief, it is the use of the Internet and social media to bring extralegal pressure, without due process, by self-described critics or social justice advocates to effect immediate and irreversible change by attacking people or charging them with wrongdoing, often in an unprincipled manner. These attacks and charges harm reputations, offer little space for reasoned rebuttal, and sometimes end careers. Yes, the use of extralegal means to achieve moral aims is sometimes useful — say, in economic boycotts or marches — but Martin Luther King and his comrades sought through moral suasion and public protest to change the law, not displace it.

Being locked out of society and being deprived of benefits and rights that one should enjoy creates the conditions for the rise of cancel culture. But in the effort to bring racial reckoning, we can't borrow ideas and behaviors that we claim to oppose. At its worst (and there is scarcely a good version), cancel culture is a proxy for white supremacy. It calls out folk one doesn't cotton to — folk whom one finds reprehensible, disgusting, or intolerable — and visits on them petulant terrors and grossly ruinous agitations. The aim is to stamp out, to eradicate, to render null and void, to erase — to, in a word, cancel. Of course, one of the problems with such loose definitions of justice is the lack of distinction. One offense is as bad as the next, or any, offense.

To be sure, when leaders with fascist leanings gripe about cancel culture, they are griping about being held even slightly accountable in a democracy whose very principles they tout but effortlessly ignore. Some powerful folk cry about the scourge of cancel culture when, for instance, they can no longer justify flying Confederate flags or praising Confederate statues as conscientious citizens bring them down. When figures who abuse power are finally brought to justice because of the words or protests of the relatively powerless, then cancel culture may seem a good thing. But those are the easy cases with straightforward results.

Precious Hadiya, I'll admit right off the bat that as an ordained Baptist preacher for more than forty years, I have been deeply rooted in a culture of compassion and a faith full of forgiveness because I — we, those of us reared in such communities — am acutely aware of my own sins, my own flaws, my own foibles, faults, and failures. I tread lightly and with great trepidation in any discussions of moral uprightness and spiritual sanctity because I know all too well how and where I have missed the mark. But one need not be religious at all to believe that we should be willing to give what we seek: charitable interpretations of behavior and a willingness to offer just appraisals of conduct with an eye toward fairness.

And while I recognize that it has ranged far beyond the Black world, cancel culture began, as do so many things, most of them good, in Black life, probably with "Black Twitter." Just as #MeToo began in Black circles and then migrated far beyond Black borders, cancel culture began as a way to bring justice and accountability to figures like singer R. Kelly and comedian Bill Cosby, who, while they had not yet been subjected to legal consequences, were subjected to an extralegal form of justice in the court of Black public opinion because of the extraordinarily long delay in bringing true justice. While those cases are clear examples of moral (and subsequently legal) concern, so many other instances of cancel culture — attacking Beyoncé for appropriating Black culture and for her views of Africa, or seeking to cancel her husband, Jay-Z, because he joined forces with the NFL to make change from within — mimic the cruelty, viciousness, and moral absolutism of the white supremacist culture Black folk despise. For this reason, as we rightly encourage white America to reckon with its complicity in systemic racism, it is also time for Black America to reckon with our self-destructive habits and not settle for fatally flawed visions in our quest for justice.

The parallels between fascist repudiations of truth and justice and those of cancel culture are hard to ignore. Our adjudicating of claims of justice on the Internet accelerated and dovetailed with the right wing's desire to destroy the rule of law. Cancel culture, whether originating in the White House or on Twitter, is the fascist refusal to recognize legitimate authority. The forces of repression are so strong and seductive that they appear on both ends of the political spectrum. As both sides are bent by social pressure, they eventually curve to form a circle. When the circle is tightened, democracy is caught in their killing circumference and dies. The presumption of cancel culture, as with fascism, is that there is a single source of truth and authority, a single understanding of what is right. There is, too, a striking similarity of means: ginning up fury and manipulating passion for the sake of linking emotion to the relief of social burdens. There is also a depressing belief in the exclusive rightness of one's cause. The fascist refusal to tolerate introspection and rigorous skepticism about the sanctity of one's beliefs is a hallmark of cancel culture as well.

Cancel culture is undeniably a judgment of our failure to address systemic and structural issues. I understand its lure to the relatively powerless: it gives the illusion that we are finally having significant movement on serious issues that keep getting delayed or denied. Is it any surprise that it is largely associated with sexism and racism, two of the biggest problems we can't seem to get a handle on?

But there is real danger in giving up in a moment of serious reckoning. The criminal justice system has too often failed women, failed to address sexual violence and much more. Cancel culture takes matters into its own hands, offering the illusion of justice. But we are confusing the manner of arriving at justice — the careful method of weighing evidence, the articulation of broad principles of agreement — with the poor outcomes we are often left with. In the end, beyond arguments about methods and means is the crucial recognition that in a true democracy, things are often messy, that you often don't get what you want or deserve immediately, and that you have to constantly engage, protest, resist, and negotiate. In short, you have to be an astute and careful citizen, like both Martin Luther King Jr. and Fannie Lou Hamer.

Precious Hadiya, cancel culture aspires to a brand of justice that occurs outside a legal arena, and I can see why. But look where we have been brought to. On the one hand, we confront an unjust legal system, one that is routinely unfair. And yet undergirding it all is a principle that might, if justly applied, yield an assessment of arguments and evidence that leads to as fair a decision as possible. There is nothing perfect, to be sure. But in many instances, figures from Thurgood Marshall to Johnnie Cochran, from Constance Baker Motley to Patricia Roberts Harris, from Pauli Murray to Benjamin Crump, have argued against nearly impossible odds and have produced favorable outcomes, or at least ones that open the way for greater justice. On the other hand, the swift judgment of extralegal moral reasoning seems to satisfy the demand for justice, but instead, too often, it only satisfies the thirst for vengeance. There is, too, a bitter realization: that we often have a better shot at justice by taking our chances on an imperfect court system than we do with cancel culture.

Precious Hadiya, those who contend that cancel culture is largely about power are right, but not necessarily in the ways they think. Ironically, many who embrace cancel culture embrace the theories of renegade figures like French philosopher Michel Foucault. But Foucault warned us that power breaks out everywhere, even between two relatively powerless folk. Power is often less Genghis Khan and more *Lord of the Flies.* As the old folk used to say, clerks run the world. If you are an applicant for SNAP (or, as they were called decades ago when I applied, food stamps), you cower in the face of the power wielded by state workers who are cogs in a bigger local or federal machine. When I went to visit my late brother in prison, my fate often rested in the hands of security guards and prison officials who could give a thumbs-up or a thumbs-down to my desire for time with him. Or, if you're trying to get into the hottest nightspot with

165

your friends, you confront a doorman who is indifferent to your pedigree or pull and can make an arbitrary decision to bar you from the premises.

There is little doubt that there are real issues of power at play, and real consequences of power at stake. Still, we must reject moral absolutism. Instead we must insist on thinking about right and wrong along a continuum of choices and a spectrum of possibilities. We must understand power as a flexible and shifting reality. Power doesn't just belong to corporate bigwigs or political elites. It belongs to everyone. Some folk grow powerful in cancel culture by swiftly judging and brutally condemning what and whom they don't like. Such critics don't even hint at the sort of impartiality that philosopher John Rawls had in mind with his thought experiment of the "original position," in which we imagine selecting moral principles to apply to all folk so that we can assign benefits or burdens as justly as possible. If we know that we or our loved ones might experience judgment, we bake as much mercy and understanding as possible into the cake of moral consequence because we know we may have to eat it one day.

It seems with cancel culture that we lack a

means of restitution or restoration, and the willingness to endure the discomfort of growth. We settle for snuffing out what we don't like. But there is no progress if we simply cancel what contradicts our beliefs or ideals. This, again, is white supremacy's methodology. Genuine racial reckoning must assume that change is still possible. The futility of cancel culture justice is that it wipes out the individual but leaves the system standing. To paraphrase sociologist Eduardo Bonilla-Silva, we end up with, for instance, misogyny without misogynists.

Revolution at its roots, the radical at its best, is usually the culmination of decades, if not centuries, of agitation that combusts in a fateful moment. And then as soon as such a movement or revolution achieves its ends, members of the revolution set out to rebuild society, establish culture, set rules, and create a culture that preserves the change it has wrought against rival claims. Now, that doesn't mean there isn't internal dialogue, strong disagreement from within, and people calling each other traitors to the cause. That sort of hyperbole has often resulted in the attempt to deny legitimacy to the "other," and that other has often been Black folk and women. Why on earth would we settle for the sort of strategies that misogyny and racism offer as the tools of trade?

If, as I have argued, cancel culture is white supremacy by proxy, it has been with us all along and is always a danger to Black people. The most obvious example for much of the nation's history is when Black men were accused of rape and subject to the noose and the lynching tree. Just the insinuation that a Black man lusted after a white woman was enough to form the mob and fetch the rope.

But there are endless examples. Kicking Black kids out of school for no good reason was, and is, cancel culture. (This is why zero-tolerance policies are cancel culture by other means, and it is one reason we shouldn't promote them, since in school, on the job, and especially at the courthouse, zero-tolerance policies work so much more powerfully against Black interests and rights than in our favor.) Killing Medgar Evers and Martin Luther King Jr. was cancel culture. Killing Malcolm X was cancel culture too, but tragically from within. And that is how white supremacy gains a foothold in Black life as we nullify each other's significance.

Precious Hadiya, I have also witnessed egregious examples of Black-on-Black disdain that is cancel culture by other names. In my own fields I have watched Black intellectuals spew venom at colleagues who were in the public eye a great deal, suggesting that their work couldn't be sufficiently rigorous or meaningful — arguments they ceased to make when they gained a little notoriety themselves. I have witnessed Black feminists rightly preach the viciousness of misogynoir and decry the patriarchy of male thinkers while treating other Black feminists with remarkable disdain. I have witnessed Black thinkers post up on social media as progressive defenders of righteous radicalism, signifying on their ideologically less faithful kin while keeping mum about seven-figure book deals and posh Ivy League teaching posts. I've witnessed preachers backbiting and denouncing their religious rivals' style of worship or speech. I've been privy to civil rights leaders pumping pure hate into the airways against a colleague's message or methods. And I've listened to writers turn needlessly snarky.

I am certainly not immune. A former mentor viciously took my name in vain and hurled epithets at me for five years in public before I decided I had no choice but to respond in a magazine essay (which took note of his virtues and his flaws, his rise and his fall) that was only a bit longer than some tweet threads I've read.

Witnessing such dispiriting intramural animosity has convinced me to go far easier on folk. I hardly agree with Kanye West, bitterly oppose his political views, and find his ideological posturing dispiriting and cynical, but I am not willing to just throw him away — nor am I willing to overlook the mental illness from which he admittedly suffers. The problem with so much of cancel culture is its insistence on the disposability of Black life, a major tenet of white supremacy. If we are to have a genuine reckoning, we can't afford to be derailed by weaponized pettiness or reactionary racial orthodoxy.

Think, for instance, of the drive to cancel the 2015 Broadway musical *Hamilton* after a filmed version of the work with the original cast debuted over the Independence Day weekend in 2020. When *Hamilton* crested the pop culture horizon in 2015, its hugely inventive attempt to deconstruct the story of the Founding Fathers by focusing on Alexander Hamilton was broadly praised. The play's creator, Lin-Manuel Miranda, of Puerto Rican descent, was inspired by the tale of an orphaned Caribbean boy born out of wedlock who eventually made his way to New York and became a Founding Father. The musical grabbed the nation by the collar near the end of the historic Obama presidency. *Hamilton* was widely viewed as an ingenious reimagining of the American story through the eyes of a lowly immigrant who became an indispensable figure in the nation's founding. It was also read in many quarters as a tribute of sorts, by happy coincidence of art and life, to the formidable remaking of American political possibility by the nation's first Black president.

But by 2020, things were dramatically different. *Hamilton* drew approving laughter from its audience in 2015 with a signature line that took a shot at the xenophobia then being whipped up by presidential candidate Donald Trump: "Immigrants, we get the job done." Yet a scant five years later, *Hamilton* was being booed and denounced for its failure to confront the nation's slave past and Hamilton's role in America's original sin. Too often, critics and the masses reacted as if *Hamilton* is a work of history, not a work of art that takes history seriously.

To be sure, there is room for artistic criticism of how *Hamilton* engaged the past — for example, about the degree to which Miranda composed his musical without an ear to the discordant notes of Hamilton's relationship to slavery. Hamilton opposed slavery and was not a slave owner, but he certainly had dealings with slave owners, like his father-in-law, and with the enslaved themselves throughout his life.

What Miranda did manage to do brilliantly is to use the artistic métier of hip hop, a linguistic innovation of the descendants of the enslaved, to articulate a pivotal moment of national becoming. He ingeniously reinterpreted the broad sweep of American political ambition, which, although it only included white men at its birth, made room in its democratic imagination for those at the bottom to remake the country in their kaleidoscopic multiracial vision. The nontraditional casting of men of color as Founding Fathers and women of color as social elites made it clear that even beyond democracy's, or the musical's, limits, this vision could be seized upon by all. To cancel such a profound artistic expression instead of wrestling with how one uses art to explore history is to confuse imagination for politics, ideology for genuine representation.

The politics of representation are a crucial element in engaging cancel culture, which is fueled as well by the sad dearth of representative ideas and images. Because there are painfully fewer creative outlets for Black folk in comparison to the dominant culture, far too big a burden is put on the television shows, plays, visual art, and books that do get circulated. And this has characterized the discussion of Black culture from the beginning of this country. When it comes to broadly circulated visual representation, the stakes are especially high — and typically contradictory. Every film must abide by strict standards and solve every issue: uplift the race but don't neglect the downtrodden, be positive and redemptive yet probe the dark dimensions of Black life, engage white supremacy but underscore Black agency, depict the trauma of slavery but show how slavery didn't exhaust our identities, renounce the politics of respectability but don't embarrass Black folk, embrace the streets but don't romanticize thugs, appreciate the diaspora but don't give too many parts to African actors.

In many instances, cancel culture involves a heated argument about Blackness — who gets the chance to define it, wear its beauty, revel in its virtues, decry the assaults on it, explore its sins, tell its truths. When it was announced that actress Cynthia Erivo would play Harriet Tubman in a major biopic, cancel culture attacked her right to the part because she is British. No one Black person or group has a copyright on a definitive expression of Blackness. We must acknowledge that there is sometimes an adoration of British identity and accents that Americans display, but that does not negate the difficulties or barriers that even British Black folk face as they seek opportunity. There is also a great deal of tension as one negotiates the world as an African Brit who has migrated to America, only to be told that one is not Black enough, or not African enough, or not authentic enough. If Denzel Washington is free to portray Caribbean characters, and Forest Whitaker and Jennifer Hudson are free to play Africans, then surely African Brits should have the freedom to portray American characters. Blackness is not a birthright to be inherited and passed on, but a precious gift that must be opened up time and again to discover all of its value.

Precious Hadiya, cancel culture rears its head in Black political life too. The noted journalist Gayle King got a bitter taste in February 2020 when she interviewed retired WNBA superstar Lisa Leslie about her recently fallen friend, basketball superstar

Kobe Bryant. Bryant had perished little more than a week earlier with his daughter Gianna (Gigi) and seven others in a helicopter crash. The fallout touched a third rail in Black life: how to speak of Black icons, especially those recently dead, when white folk are looking and listening. King asked Leslie if the sexual assault allegations against Bryant from a decade and a half earlier would tarnish his legacy. Because huge swaths of Black America were still mourning his death, her questions provoked great anger and vocal outrage. But there is a greater lesson in figuring out why his death and this controversy impacted us as they did.

To begin with, our mourning was sparked by sheer admiration for Kobe's enormous physical gifts, his athletic domination, which, while he was alive, he maximized, perhaps more so than most of the players to whom he could be compared. And while he hadn't played professionally in more than three years when he died, he would appear at games, flash that magnetic smile, give a brotherly pound to Lakers superstar LeBron James, offer counsel in the stands to Gigi, his precious prodigy daughter who was destined to be great like he was great. Now he, and tragically she too, was gone.

We mourned his loss, and in mourning Kobe, we mourned ourselves. All grieving is a bit selfish — well, maybe more than a bit; perhaps it is even a lot selfish. We mourned the passing from the scene of the man who, because of those gifts, gave us so many thrilling memories. Yes, we grieved because he had died too young, and that meant that we would no longer witness a body that not so long ago exhibited a dynamic drive for greatness, an unquenchable thirst to be the best ever, an unshakable self-confidence, a zealous, unapologetic, monomaniacal commitment to craft.

We mourned because we would no longer be able to remark upon how gracefully he was aging, how he was preserving the beauty of face and limb that marked his transcendent run for two decades. We would no longer be able to see what magic he would conjure next from his body. The body that he had inconceivably willed to get up from the floor after tearing his Achilles tendon and then take two free throws before hobbling back to the locker room to begin the arduous and nearly impossible journey back to playing again. He ended his career with an unimaginable flourish of sixty points in his final game. Even before that, Kobe learned how to shoot the ball differently after he fractured his right index finger — and still competed for a championship. It added to his legend that he won his final ring in 2010 with a broken finger. Kobe left it all, always, on the floor.

That's why we miss him; that's why we mourned him. That stubborn, won't-lose, can't-be-defeated, iron will that adjusts and improvises in the face of challenge and opposition inspired millions of us to keep going in the face of our own difficulties. Kobe had taken to telling stories through film with the same passion and imagination he displayed on the court. When he died, we were just getting a taste of his gifts as a chronicler of culture.

And we were just beginning to discover new personal dimensions of Kobe when he died. We mourned the loss of a man who loved his home life even more than he'd once loved his hardwood exploits. We mourned him as the father of four daughters, especially as he took his second-oldest daughter, Gigi, under his wing and nurtured her hoops hopes and her gift for ball. We mourned the loss of a man who matured and evolved, a man who set a clear example of how to transition from love of game to love of his girls, and, by extension, love of other girls and women in a culture where such love had been sadly segregated by gender and often quarantined to the domestic sphere. We seem to appreciate women more in gowns and heels than in jerseys and sneakers. We mourned his loss because a genuine champion of women's sports died.

All of this was at play, precious Hadiya, when Gayle King engaged Kobe's dear friend Lisa Leslie. King's interview with Leslie touched on how Kobe lovingly mimicked Michael Jordan in his play, how he significantly boosted women's basketball games by his avid attendance, and his pride and love for his daughter Gigi. Near the three-minute mark of their five-minute conversation, King asked her controversial question about Bryant. Leslie contended that Kobe wasn't the sort of person to violate a woman. King pushed back and suggested that Leslie wouldn't see that side of Kobe because he was her friend. Leslie admitted that it was possible even though she didn't believe Kobe was guilty of assault.

Many Black folk were angry that King raised the question at all. And yet that misunderstands the role of a journalist. Although King should surely be sensitive to the situation, her role is not to advocate for one point of view or the other. Her job is to

get to the truth as best she can while prob-
ing the facts as she understands them.
Despite some claims, journalists certainly
can't be objective. They can't stand outside
the scope of human experience as neutral
observers. But they can nevertheless be fair
by showing a principled regard for evidence
and offering a nuanced interpretation of the
case before them. King raised the allegations because they were so public and
because they are directly relevant to how
Kobe might be perceived by the broader
society.

In so doing, King permitted Leslie to
expound on Kobe's virtues and to insist on
his innocence. Had King not asked the
question, Leslie wouldn't have had the
chance to offer a reasonable defense of her
beloved friend. Such a defense may not have
seemed necessary to most of Black America.
But it is one that may have spoken to those
beyond the Black world who harbored
skepticism of or outright hostility for Bryant.

Gayle King's question was actually a
conduit for the claim of Kobe's moral
uprightness and a defense of Kobe's reputation that King couldn't — and shouldn't —
make as a journalist. What those who were
angry at King missed is that she sent a big
fat pitch down the middle of the plate, and

Leslie knocked it right out of the park. King allowed one of Kobe's most skillful defenders to have her say to a sometimes doubtful white world. The blunt edge of cancel culture did not recognize the subtle meanings at play.

Other Black folk were aggrieved that the allegation of sexual assault had been isolated from the cultural and racial forces that helped make the charge credible for many. Kobe was charged with sexual assault as a twenty-four-year-old in 2003 in Eagle, Colorado, an overwhelmingly white city, by a nineteen-year-old white female employee at the elite spa he was staying at in preparation for knee surgery. The relations between Black men and white women have historically been fraught and have often been conducted in secrecy. In our nation's history, a white woman's charge of rape by a Black man was not infrequently used to cover, or even deny, a socially taboo attraction. For many white women a tryst or sexual relationship with a Black man meant claims of racial disloyalty and the betrayal of white men. And many white women were willing to sacrifice Black male safety for their own cultural security.

That history, plus the trial of O. J. Simpson, accused of murdering his white ex-wife less than a decade before, weighed heavily on the minds of Black folk witnessing the potential demise of a clean-cut, well-spoken, multilingual Renaissance man like Kobe. When his accuser refused to testify, the charges were dropped. A civil suit was later filed and settled out of court, which included Bryant issuing an apology to the young woman without an admission of guilt.

It angered many Blacks when white actress Evan Rachel Wood tweeted hours after Kobe's death: "What has happened is tragic. I am heartbroken for Kobe's family. He was a sports hero. He was also a rapist. And all of these truths can exist simultaneously." In the minds of many Black folk, though hardly all, the case against Bryant was neither legally clear-cut nor morally compelling. While it seems there was clearly a sexual experience, many Blacks believed it was consensual. Still, Bryant's apology admitted in retrospect that the young woman perceived the encounter differently.

The case against Kobe existed in the sexual climate that predated the #MeToo movement, when we were not as sensitive to rape culture as we are now. But Black folk can hardly agree with one critical consequence of #MeToo — that to be charged with a crime is to be in effect found guilty. That has been the backbone of grave injustice done to Black folk who met their demise at the end of a rope. Black anger at the attempt to relitigate Kobe's case more than a decade after its legal resolution — a legal process that has often not benefited Black folk — is stoked by centuries of oppression and injustice. Kobe caught the backdraft of the movement in 2018 when seventeen thousand people unsuccessfully petitioned to revoke his Academy Award nomination for his animated short "Dear Basketball." He won the Oscar in 2018. But a petition to remove him as a juror from the 2018 Animation Is Film Festival prevailed. Signatories claimed that Kobe was an "accused rapist and sexual predator." When he was removed by the film jury, he said that the decision "further motivates me and my commitment to building a studio that focuses on diversity and inclusion in storytelling for the animation industry."

Wood's tweeted verdict, delivered in the hours after Kobe's tragic death, rang out as a harsh rebuke to those who claimed him as icon and hero. Unlike King's journalistic dive into the matter, which opened space for a countervailing narrative, this was a one-sided condemnation. Wood's tweet was in league with *Washington Post* reporter Felicia Sonmez tweeting out an article about Bryant's sexual assault case right after his death. Sonmez, a survivor of sexual assault, no doubt was driven by her experience to post the article. It is legitimate to ask whether Sonmez's gesture, for which she was suspended, was an act of responsible journalism or an understandable personal reaction that nevertheless reflected tainted judgment.

It is also clear that victims of sexual violence were triggered by Kobe's death because in many of their minds he represented a victimizer, an assaulter. We must understand their pain and acknowledge their trauma. Our culture has so completely failed victims of sexual assault and violence that high-profile figures like Bryant, no matter their arguable innocence, become a ready vehicle for — in truth, an avatar of — the shameful abuse of women. Thus, even a case as complicated as Kobe's becomes an outlet to symbolically prosecute other cases that are far clearer and yet don't get pursued or resolved. In a sense, this makes King's questioning an even more compelling example of principled and useful journalism, especially in light of a huge racial divide in perception that is still at play. While 40 percent of whites were "very" or "somewhat" sympathetic to Bryant at the time of his case, nearly two-thirds of Black folk felt that way. That racial gap in perception doesn't seem to have closed much since then.

Where King may be vulnerable to criticism is when she suggested that Leslie might be incapable of acknowledging Kobe's potential guilt because she was his friend. King's suggestion seemed spontaneous and was perhaps a commonsense conclusion drawn from observation of human nature or other instances where proximity blunts perspective. But that very metric could as easily be turned against King herself: her own closeness to deposed former co-anchor Charlie Rose — who lost his post because of sexual harassment allegations — was apparent when she said, "I know there are two sides to every story, that's what I know." Yet what King took away in that statement to Lisa she more than gave back when she asked her if it was even fair to talk about Bryant in this way because he was "no longer with us," and because the case had been resolved. King's sharpest cancel culture critics missed how she aired doubt about her very premise.

What we also overlook is the mainstream white media's failure to portray Black life in its glorious complexity. The white media has often been oblivious to racial nuance, or ignorant of and indifferent to the distorted ways that society has perceived Black folk. Thus, any criticism, valid or not, aimed at Black folk is usually rejected and seen as tantamount to further eviscerating our humanity. The belief that Black heroes and icons have a rough go of it in the white media is not difficult to understand — just look at the sometimes harsh and unfair light cast on figures as different as Jack Johnson and Malcolm X, Eartha Kitt and Shirley Sherrod, Marcus Garvey and Martin Luther King Jr. As we undertake a national racial reckoning, the white media must be closely examined and taken to task for its many failures. Even as the American media rightly decries its vicious mistreatment by a paranoid, delusional, racist, and neofascist president like Trump, it must acknowledge how it, too, has severely missed the mark on race.

The impulse to protect our racial heroes and cultural saints is understandable. But Black protectionism has also been extended to questionable or undeserving figures. For instance, long after Bill Cosby was tried and convicted of sexual assault, many Black folk argued that he was a victim of white supremacy or a conspiracy of powerful whites to take him out because he was on the verge of purchasing NBC. It is not surprising, though no less appalling, that Cosby, from jail, tweeted his thanks to venerable rapper Snoop Dogg for the latter's epithet-laced video lashing of Gayle King for the question about Kobe's assault charge — a video that also seemed to imply a threat of physical violence. Snoop later apologized and said that he neither intended nor wished any harm to King. The waves of misogyny unleashed on King were deeply disturbing. The hate and threats were way out of proportion to any offense she may have given. Although these sorts of assaults surely preceded cancel culture, such brisk expressions of venom often blanket social media as enraged participants direct their ire in unforgiving terms. This sort of poisonous attack can ignite dangerous and destructive consequences — from the annihilation of reputation to bodily harm.

It seems lost on those most angry with King that Kobe had his own moments of complicated Black response, of evolving Black consciousness. Bryant once chafed at the box into which Black athletes are cast. "And it's always a struggle to step outside of that," he said to the *New Yorker* in 2014.

When he was asked about LeBron James posting online a stark, moving photo of himself and fellow Miami Heat players donning hoodies in solidarity with the tragically killed Trayvon Martin, Kobe declared, "I won't react to something just because I'm supposed to, because I'm an African American. That argument doesn't make any sense to me." He said, "If we've progressed as a society, then you don't jump to somebody's defense just because they're African American. You sit and you listen to the facts just like you would in any situation, right? So I won't assert myself."

I reached out to Kobe to lovingly but firmly disagree with him. Sports journalist Jemele Hill criticized Kobe on ESPN as tone-deaf, prompting him to reach out to her by phone. Kobe argued that he had been wrongfully accused of sexual assault, which initially made him sympathetic to Trayvon's accused murderer, George Zimmerman. But Kobe eventually changed his mind; he met with Trayvon's family and apologized to them, and he spoke at a rally for the fallen teen a year after Zimmerman had been acquitted of his murder. That's the Kobe Bryant I knew: a man willing to think for himself, willing to admit his error, willing to grow and evolve.

The question must be posed: How might a restored, redeemed man look if he changes his life and moves toward the goal of healthy masculinity? In the wake of the charges in Colorado, Kobe composed a life that trended decidedly toward self-reflection and self-correction, toward maturing and becoming a better human being — the very moral arc for which any notion of restorative justice should aim.

Precious Hadiya, we should be willing to practice patience and forgiveness. We should be willing to tolerate views that run counter to our own, to talk to people who look and sound like enemies, to not close our ears to what we don't want to hear, to openly debate ideas, even those we find offensive. We should be willing to pit our learning and rhetoric against folk and speech we find repulsive. Still, we must also always grapple with the racial and gender complications, histories, and perspectives I have here tried to elaborate.

We also need a solid and compelling notion of racial amnesty. Otherwise potential allies are tragically made into implacable enemies. We should not witch-hunt our way through the racial pasts of white folk, seeking to discover if and where they've erred. If folk own up to the fact they haven't got this race thing right — that they're willing to try to be better, and that they will, with the help of those who care to aid them, find a better path and more healing tone to their speech and lives, their thoughts and behavior — we shouldn't be ready to scratch them off the list. If Virginia governor Ralph Northam dressed up in blackface, yes, hold him to account, but, please God, don't cancel him. Let him stay in office. There is no better ally to Black folk than a white man in power who tastes forgiveness and appreciates a second chance to get things right. And Northam's increased focus on the theme of racial justice, including attention to maternal mortality and equity in transportation and funding for black colleges, and his actions since — including the effort to change how public schools teach racial history, the removal of a Robert E. Lee statue in Richmond, and the restoration of the voting rights of ten thousand former felons, which disproportionately benefits Black folk — have proved this is true. If justice is what love sounds like when it speaks in public, then patience is what mercy sounds like out loud, and forgiveness is the accent with which grace speaks. None of this means that white folk don't face a huge moment of reckoning. How they handle this can shape the nation's history for years to come.

But when it comes to black life in America, there's only one conclusion I can reach about some white people: You don't care to put yourself in our shoes. The consequences of this lack of imagination for black Americans are deadly. . . . If you don't have much interest in how we live and love, you'll never understand what we're fighting to preserve. . . . White people have never needed to exercise that kind of curiosity. You've never had to. You can live your whole lives without really considering how we live ours. We, on the other hand, know you very well. We've had to. We had no choice.

— KASI LEMMONS

Our freedom keeps being dismantled and limited because of white comfort.

— TRACEE ELLIS ROSS

# 5. WHITE COMFORT

Dear Sandra Bland,
Of all the stories about police brutality that have come to us over the last few years, your story, for a number of reasons, is among the most disconcerting. I don't know quite how to say this, since I recognize that times have changed and I'm a Black man of a certain age with a certain outlook, but it angers me greatly that this big white southern cop felt free to manhandle you. Yes, I realize that I may be accused of an outdated sense of manhood or misplaced chivalry, or even that I'm flashing signs of toxic masculinity and missing the larger issue of your moral autonomy and female agency, but at the end of the day, when I see the videos of your encounter, I find myself saying to the bully cop, "Pick on somebody your own size. Or at least your own gender." But of course it doesn't matter if you're big enough to fight back. What matters is the circumstance, and

the circumstance with cops is that they always have the gun, the badge, the baton, the authority, and the official stamp of approval. And when they kill you, they have qualified immunity plus the unqualified support of the state and much of the white public, which just can't seem to understand that we are sick to our souls from the repeated cycle of death at the hands of cops.

Every time I watch videos of your arrest — well, really, your assault — I'm proud of the fact that you gave as good as you got, that you stood up for yourself with high intelligence, biting sarcasm, and lacerating signifying, trying to shame the cop for his heedless ambush of a Black woman who knew her way around a phrase and knew how to cut to the heart of the matter. Your presence clearly made the cop uncomfortable, no matter how reasonable you tried to be. In fact, your reasoning skills seemed to have irked him even more. You would have had in that instant to become an entirely different being, undergone an ontological makeover that would have made Heidegger or Sartre or even Fanon marvel, in order to escape his wrath. Most white folk fail to get this when they ask, "Why don't you just cooperate?" Besides the fact that most of us do cooperate, as countless videos prove, there's the larger issue of how one must suddenly contort one's bodily expressions and fold one's entire history and being into a made-for-white-comfort presentation: the Black person speaks when spoken to, says things loudly enough to be heard but not too loudly. The margin of error is extremely tight in such high-octane situations. It's just all too much.

My dear Sandra, in the end your moral beauty spoke through your outrage and your utter contempt for an absurdity that most Black folk have made peace with but which you refused to accept — being stopped and then badly mistreated and physically assaulted for a failure to signal. Your death reveals the cost of such bravery, not just for you, but for countless Black lives made to repeat such rituals of survival time and again, to the point where microaggressions don't seem so micro at all. We wonder about the ability to maintain equilibrium.

You were stopped and arrested on a Friday in July 2015 after you had just driven a thousand miles from Chicago to take a job at Prairie View A&M. It was to start the following Monday, but you didn't have the $500 for bail. Just three days later, you were found hanging in your cell, with the official conclusion that you committed suicide. It is tragic whatever the case may be: whether somebody snuffed your life and made it look like suicide or your ordeal caused such depression and triggered such mental duress that you decided you could no longer abide the situation. It is tragic that you were unjustly locked up to begin with.

Dear Sandra, your interaction with that state trooper reminds us of something that for too long has been ignored. It is a truth we have to confront amidst our national racial reckoning: so much of Black and Brown life, and that of Indigenous and Asian folk, too, has been lived with the imperative to reinforce white comfort. Yes, white privilege, white innocence, and white fragility are real and must be acknowledged and grappled with. But we must also confront white comfort, which is basically the arrangement of the social order for the convenience of white folk, one that offers them comfort as a noun, that is, ease and relief from pain or limits or constraints, and comfort as a verb, that is, taking action to console white grief or distress.

When you think of it, so much of the nation has been built to establish and preserve white comfort. Slavery existed to provide white folk enormous comfort — providing all the energy needed to maintain farms and plantations. Black folk did all of this to support the nation's bottom line as white folk collectively reaped untold financial benefits and the American economy grew to monstrous proportions. Jim Crow, and in many ways white life ever since, was constructed for white comfort: to keep Blacks and others from drinking at the same water fountains, eating at the same restaurants, riding on the same buses, sitting in the same classrooms, playing on the same diamonds, gridirons, or courts, worshiping in the same sanctuaries, and, God forbid, being buried in the same cemeteries, all because white folk believed that they were superior and that they should be spared the discomfort of having to be near what and whom they were better than. And, just in case their heightened view of themselves proved to be false, they spared themselves the discomfort of confronting the ugly truth. Thus they protected themselves from any contradictions of or challenges to these notions. Where the South's brand of de jure segregation didn't work, the North's de facto separation proved just as good. White folk were comforted, and that comfort kept them from knowing too much of anything that was worth knowing about Black life.

The immortal Fannie Lou Hamer explains how the delusional sense of white superiority deprived white folk of the kind of knowledge of Black life that Black folk had to have of the white world just to survive. White folk outsmarted themselves by placing us in an inferior position, she argues, because we got the epistemic drop on the white world. "I'm going to put it on the line, because my job is not to make people feel comfortable," Hamer said.

> You've been caught up in this thing because . . . [t]here's nothing under the sun that made you believe that you was just like me, that under this white pigment of skin is red blood, just like under this black skin of mine. . . . You had been put on a pedestal, and then not only put on a pedestal, but you had been put in something like a[n] ivory castle. White Americans today don't know what in the world to do because when they put us behind them, that's where they made their mistake. If they had put us in front, they wouldn't have let us look back. But they put us behind them, and we watched every move they made.

Earlier in her speech, Hamer punctures

the myth of white superiority and tramples on the illusion that white folk worked as hard as Black folk. Both of her assertions are gravely discomforting to the white status quo. She argues that white folk must be thrust into the sort of struggle — for knowledge, for self-awareness, for understanding of how the world works — that Black folk have had to wage from the beginning of our time here. Because we were deemed invisible, we were treated to a front-row seat to the rites and rituals of white culture. Because we were deemed stupid, we were able to absorb intelligence about white plans and secretly pass them along to other Black folk in a position to make use of such knowledge in all kinds of Black freedom struggles.

If, as millions of white folks now say, the jig is up, the time is at hand, the day of reckoning is upon us, then white comfort must go — the comfort of depending on our kindness and tempered rage; the comfort of swift reassurance that while things are pretty bad, in the bigger racial scheme you're not that bad; the comfort of believing that a few quick symbolic changes here and a few quick personal adjustments there will solve everything; and the comfort that after a few bruising months things will get back to normal. But the racial pandemic, much like the global health pandemic, has changed some things forever.

Dear Sandra, I hardly need to tell you that one of the greatest white comforts is not having to know anything about Black life. There is little pressure to know its epic sweep and narrative grandeur, its political struggle and social triumph, its moral heroism and existential courage, its intellectual complexity and its transcendent cultural trajectory, all met by relentless resistance and outright hostility from a myriad of white forces. It is the Black "next" up against the white "again" in every arena, over and over again. Some white folk have deemed the study of Black life and history uninteresting. Some whites claim it is irrelevant to the larger American narrative, arguing that Black folk didn't have much to do with shaping the events of our history. Some whites were never taught a sense of Black achievement in class or at home. Others are unapologetically anti-Black and disdain the study of Black life. Still others boast a negative literacy about Black life, what might be called an ill-literacy, in which the point of studying Black life is to take measure of its supposed social corruption and moral depravity — to prove through myopic statistics that Black folk are plagued by greater social pathology, commit more crime, are less interested in education, don't behave well in public, are psychologically toxic and intellectually inferior, have dysfunctional family structures, ruin neighborhoods with their questionable values, and deserve their low status in society.

Black life and history are rarely explored at length in grade schools or even in advanced placement courses in high school. The likes of James Baldwin or Toni Morrison may squeak through, but the prospect of white students becoming familiar with W. E. B. Du Bois or Anna Julia Cooper seems awfully slim. Slavery remains a controversial and largely neglected, or at times severely redacted, course of study in many schools. Jim Crow is a murky chapter in history that is broached delicately if at all. The Civil War is still too often taught in the context of bitter disputes over states' rights, and Reconstruction gets short shrift and sometimes is presented as a period when we were all equal. The civil rights movement is basically reduced to the "I Have a Dream" speech by Martin Luther King Jr. And Barack Obama becomes a colorful coda in books that have caught up to the recent past, while those who forged his political path, figures such as William Dawson, Charles Diggs, Shirley Chisholm, Carol Moseley Braun, and the formidable Jesse Jackson, whose historic presidential runs in 1984 and 1988 cleared away big electoral hurdles for Obama, are barely mentioned.

Sports stars get a little shine. White fans appreciate people like Jesse Owens and Jackie Robinson, but not so much the late-sixties- and early-seventies-era Muhammad Ali, who bravely dressed down America's racial hypocrisy. To the extent that many white folk learn anything about Black culture through its athletes and entertainers, they view them much the way the character Pino did in the classic Spike Lee film *Do the Right Thing.* When Lee's character, Mookie, quizzes Pino about his favorite basketball player, movie star, and rock star, they're all Black: Magic Johnson, Eddie Murphy, and Prince, though Pino insists he prefers Bruce Springsteen. "Pino, all you ever talk about is nigger this and nigger that, and all your favorite people are so-called niggers," Mookie says. Pino tries to explain it away: "It's different. Magic, Eddie, Prince are not niggers. I mean, they're not Black. I mean — let me explain myself . . . They're more than Black. It's different."

Even without holding Pino's explicitly racist views, many whites believe they're doing a good thing when they single out Black folk for having traits they don't normally associate with Blackness: hard work, clean character, sparkling intelligence. But that says more about white folk than Black folk. Thus, to compliment some Black folk for showcasing excellence in a number of pursuits is to tell on one's skepticism that Black culture is the breeding ground for such habits and traits. These figures and features of Black life are seen as "more than Black" — not typically Black, hence not representatively Black, and thus not really Black at all. Black pathology is seen as an extension of Black identity; Black excellence is seen as its exception. Caught between stereotypes and vast ignorance, many whites find that their knowledge of Black life is severely limited. In sharp contrast, most Black folk are hardly surprised, though always proud, that Black people are diligent, ethical, and smart.

Dear Sandra, if white folk are serious about the siege of ignorance coming to an end, the sort of ignorance that helped to end your life, then they've got to put themselves into uncomfortable circumstances; they must reject the comfort of ignoring the raw Black truth that Black folk must live with. Such learning doesn't happen overnight; it can't be done in a CliffsNotes version of Black identity. White brothers and sisters must deliberately expose themselves to experiences that force them to grow. They've got to swim in the pools of our thoughts and expressions, our resistance and rebellion, our tragedies and traumas, our arguments and disagreements, our joys and affections, our love and happiness.

The immersion in Black life and thought is often a difficult task. We got a hint of this during Barack Obama's first run for the presidency, when excerpts from sermons by his former pastor Jeremiah Wright surfaced. Things didn't go well. America was offered a sonic drive-by of a legendary pulpiteer who distinguished himself in a culture teeming with rhetorical genius. Wright was long revered because his sermons gleamed with the poetry of a prophet imbued with sacred imagination, colorful exegesis of scripture, tremendous interpretive powers, and the ability to link Black folk and pop cultures to the Word.

A snippet emerged from one of Wright's sermons where he, in context, spoke about the nation repeating the phrase "God bless America." Wright insisted that the opposite was true: that in light of the nation's many offenses and injustices to people of color and others, God wouldn't dare bless our unholy mess. Rather, we should say "God damn America," because this nation bucked God's will and undercut a just vision of democracy. Prophets routinely use rhetorical excess and verbal exaggeration to drive home a theologically resonant point. If white folk had spent any time in the Black church and listened to the social gospel preached by some of the greatest preachers in the land — from the pulpits of Frederick Haynes III and Gina Stewart, Otis Moss III and Jawanza Colvin, Lance Watson and Rudolph McKissick, Cynthia Hale and Howard-John Wesley, Solomon Kinloch and Carlyle Fielding Stewart III, Marcus Cosby and Neichelle Guidry, Claudette Copeland and T. D. Jakes — they would hardly have been surprised to hear criticism of the nation from Wright. If they had sat in such sanctuaries over the years, they would have absorbed the powerful prophecy and heard the uplifting self-help, and taken in the strong resistance to white nationalism while affirming a profound love of country.

Or take some of the first words as president about police and Black communities from Wright's former parishioner Barack

Obama. They came after the infamous legal incident with Harvard professor Henry Louis Gates Jr. — Gates had returned home from China to discover his door was jammed; his driver helped him gain entry to the house; a passerby suspecting a break-in called the police; there was a conflict between Gates and the responding officer that led to Gates's arrest; and finally there occurred a national debate about race and law enforcement. President Obama commented at a press conference, "I think it's fair to say, number one, any of us would be pretty angry; number two, that the Cambridge police acted stupidly in arresting somebody when there was already proof that they were in their own home; and, number three, what I think we know separate and apart from this incident is that there's a long history in this country of African Americans and Latinos being stopped by law enforcement disproportionately. That's just a fact."

There has rarely been a more reasonable and balanced voice on Black folk and law enforcement than President Obama. He went out of his way to show support of law enforcement and the exceedingly tough jobs they had in serving and protecting the public even as he argued for the most commonsensical reforms to police departments to ensure justice for Black folk. In the case of Gates, Obama acknowledged the anger any citizen would feel if they had been treated like Gates that day. There was great anger over Obama's supposed disrespect for law enforcement when all he did was make a simple declarative statement that any reasonable mind would agree is true. Despite his attempt to gently but directly address the mammoth hurts and simmering hostilities between Black folk and the cops, the reactive white discomfort kept him for a while from touching again the third rail of race and prevented white Americans from learning about Blackness in its complex varieties from one of the sharpest minds in the land. That was more than a little disconcerting to Black folk because we realized that if America couldn't listen to the truth from Obama, then few other voices stood a chance.

The work of listening and learning is deep and long. Only when white folk are willing to come in among Black folk and see us in the varied scenes and contradictory situations that constitute Black existence can they begin to discern the shape and contours of our culture. And, of course, reading deeply from the wealth of scholarly reflection on our pilgrimage in America is crucial to reckoning with white comfort. There has been a spate of books about our racial crisis, and they should be inhaled as well.

And, dear Sandra, it is only natural that after waking up, white brothers and sisters want to share that awakening. But the comfort of being awakened on someone else's dime, on someone else's back, or, in the case of George Floyd, on someone else's neck, must be brought up short with the realization that no matter how sincere such awakening is, it has arrived far into the history of Black people and our culture and struggle in this nation. Often between Black folk and white folk there is a mismatch of enthusiasms and an incompatibility of social efforts, even as there is appreciation for the possibility of change. But the dark skepticism that sometimes grows in quarters of Black America is fed by a constant cycle of the mini-awakenings of white America — briefly during and after slavery, at points during Jim Crow, after civil rights struggles in the sixties, after the election of the first Black president — and the unwillingness to sustain the discomfort necessary for true growth and partnership.

Another way of saying this is that while white folk are in many instances just waking up, Black folk have been awake — "woke" — for centuries, and although that's a necessary virtue, it's also a huge burden. We have been under attack for so long that we dare not close our eyes even for a minute. We have had one long case of racial insomnia, watching over our families and communities, protecting them until a morning that never seems to come because there's always some other nightfall descending, some other consequence of white comfort that keeps us on the run, on the watch — say, a dislike for affirmative action because it makes white folk uncomfortable to give up even a little unearned advantage, or a disdain for Black neighbors and the discomfort of encountering Black faces while fetching the morning paper. And when we managed to catch a few winks, our sleep was either riddled with nightmares or interrupted by the alarming persistence of defenders of white comfort railing against the quest for Black relief.

It is a way of saying that many Black folk are exhausted: worn out by the cumulative injuries, quiet indignities, loud assaults, existential threats, microaggressions, macro offenses, and unceasing bombarding of our bodies and psyches in the name of white comfort. Many of us would love nothing more than to take a nap and leave white folk to clean up the mess made by centuries of white comfort. That, too, is a form of dreaming while awake, or daydreaming — the only kind of dreaming we can afford. This is why Langston Hughes strung together magical words of poetry about dreaming and why Martin Luther King Jr. dreamed out loud for the world to hear in Washington, D.C., in 1963. This is why King was forever tired, his weary southern cadence haunted by the somber melodies of sleeplessness. King's lieutenant Andrew Young said he waged "a war on sleep." King warned the nation of the difficulty of "Remaining Awake Through a Great Revolution," although he was made sleepless by his worry that white folk wouldn't create a just society. King realized that his life was too great a luxury for the guardians of white comfort, mostly because his dream didn't stop in 1963 but rather led him to far more radical visions of economic justice. Like King, most of us must maintain what runaway slave and abolitionist William Parker called "sleepless vigilance."

This sheer Black exhaustion sometimes sounds like cranky disregard for white awakening when in fact it may only be our refusal to any longer consider white comfort. It is also the old recurring fear that this awakening may not last, that even though this time seems different, it may not be. White folk won't really stick with the hard work of genuinely reckoning with the racist past, and therefore we don't want to get too invested — we don't want to get our hopes up too much. Our cynicism may indeed be a form of hurt, of pain, of racial world-weariness, of emotional depletion, and of soul deflation that comes out as anger or even rage — a rage that is still hopeful because it believes that rage might make a difference.

Dear Sandra, in order for white folk to surrender comfort and claim a true awakening, they must hear and not be defensive about Black claims of exhaustion. And, come to think of it, there is (quite literally in the spelling, but of course also in the meanings, beyond etymology, that we bring to the word from the depth of our experience and imagination) rage at the heart of mirage, which is what results when the white illusion that things aren't as bad as we know they are wins out over our descriptions of the hurt and pain we see. There is rage in tragedy, when our enormous anger is sparked by the racial catastrophe and chaos

211

we endure. But there is rage in courage, too, where we are motivated by our rage at the dying of the light to be braver than we might ordinarily be and to forge ahead and make things happen with our energy and determination. And, yes, there is rage in encouragement, too, because when we are disgusted at injustice, we war against it while uplifting the spirits of those who are its greatest victims.

There are plenty of Black folk who claim exhaustion. They say they aren't here to serve white folk, not here to educate them, not here to uplift them or to guide them on the path of racial righteousness. They think that is just another way to preserve white comfort and that the most effective way for white folk to overcome their dependence on Blackness is to learn to swim without the aid of Black lifeguards.

Beneath that Black exhaustion is a sound reason and wide-awake rationale for such a stance. After all, the argument goes, if white folk really wanted to learn about race, they could have done so long before now. What can we teach them that they haven't already been able to learn? What can we say that hasn't already been said?

One reason many Black folk are resentful of teaching white folk is that we have found ourselves in that position all too often. We have often had to teach them jobs when they were starting out, and then, when they learned, they were promoted and we were stuck in place. Or, in a variation of the theme, our idea for a project at work got turned down before we shared it with a white person who ran with it and won acclaim — just as in class our comments were often ignored while white students who repeated our sentiments garnered approval. There may be a muscle memory and culturally ingrained reflex in this resistance. Some Black folk are upset because not learning about white folk was never an option for us. All of our learning drew from the shared knowledge and common wisdom that we passed along to each other. What white folk sought to teach us was more like propaganda, and we viewed that through our own instincts and intuitions, through our own common sense, and we drew our own conclusions. We have often been highly skeptical of the official white narrative.

Some Black folk are resentful of white authors, activists, and experts on race who, riding the wave of white wokeness, end up re-centering whiteness — because white grief, shame, or guilt over past sins leads them to decry their unfortunate, even tragic exercise of privilege. Thus, racial absolution highlights the bruised or repentant white person, and before you know it the conversation ceases to be about social change and racial justice, and the offending whiteness is once again at the center, while Blackness, as usual, is playing in the background. There is real hurt involved: while Black folk are the true inspiration for woke white writers, they are denied the cultural legitimacy and financial windfall such folk reap once they hit the circuits to tell white folk to stop being white in the ways that Black writers have been saying for centuries.

It should not have to be said, but Black folk are not all the same. We don't all think the same thoughts about Blackness, we don't all agree about the approaches to heal racial injustice, we don't all think the same way about white folk and their roles in movements for justice. There are many Black folk who draw inspiration from the gospel lyric "I don't feel no ways tired" or, from another song, "I'm not tired yet." To be fair, even those who claim utter exhaustion aren't always as tired as they think they are, or as tired as they tell others they are, since the very announcement of such exhaustion is meant as much to encourage white folk to do some homework as it is to report an objective state of being. Some folk who are truly tired can still find ways to dig deeper and to keep going.

A powerful source of exhaustion is that many of our kids to whom we have taught our culture or who have otherwise learned about it are drafted to share that knowledge with their fellow white students in their high school and college classes. They often end up serving as unofficial teachers, something that eats up time they could spend on learning or enjoying themselves in other pursuits. And then should some of those Black students fall behind, they are blamed for not being able to keep up. All of their hard work to educate their fellow students is ignored and not appreciated. Schools often use Black students in this way in order to achieve racial reckoning on the cheap. They avoid bringing in teachers — or, in other settings, corporations avoid bringing in experts — to address gaps, holes, and areas of ignorance. And the burden for teaching falls on the few Black or Brown folk in the room or office, instead of being assumed by the white folk in those arenas in need of the reflection and change. It is all so utterly exhausting.

Still, dear Sandra, there are some Black folk who are determined in this moment of reckoning to do whatever they can to help white folk get their racial act together. These Black folk will help in any way they can if white folk ask sincerely because they actually want to know. They take white folk at their word to further encourage them to do better. On the surface, this seems like catering to white comfort and endorsing the absence of the very unease that is the spur to growth. And that may indeed be true in some instances. But there are many occasions when something else is at work, that is, a Black willingness to support the effort, or, in the vernacular of the moment, to help them become a better "white ally."

These sorts of Black folk are keen on separating substantive white engagement with the issue of racism and anti-Black attitudes from what is now termed performative empathy, which is all for show and not to grow. But in adopting new language for social change, we must be careful not to shun important meanings from the past. I've always been partial to a more holistic idea of performance. After all, without theater and dramaturgy, John Lewis couldn't have helped to forge an immortal march against the shock troopers of bigotry on the Edmund Pettus Bridge. Nor could Martin Luther King Jr. have made as compelling a case for the integration of Birmingham without the dramatic violence of water hoses and police dogs being unleashed on Black activists. In each case the strategic use of performance — on a bridge, or with dogs and fire hoses — led to substantive changes. For King and a host of others, it was the passage of the Civil Rights Act in 1964, and for Lewis and a great cloud of witnesses, it was the passage of the Voting Rights Act of 1965. Although we are undeniably tired, we shouldn't sleep on the power of performance and the use of the symbolic to enact real social change.

Dear Sandra, white folk must get to know us well enough not to be thrown off by the vigorous differences and family shouting matches that often emerge in our communities. Black folk can be just as ornery and nasty with each other as any other group of folks can be, even when we're on the same side of the fight. Becoming a true ally of the Black fight for social justice means that white folk abide by a credo that complements the one that has served Black folk well: know your white folk. In this instance, white folk must know their Black folk. They must know the kinds of Black folk with whom they get along, who push and challenge them, who insist that they do their best, who offer them tough love and straight talk, who get squarely in the face of their white comfort and unmask its pretensions to solidarity even as it holds to unspoken privileges, unacknowledged biases, and unearned reassurances.

Dear Sandra, although the love should be tough, it should also be appropriately tender and understanding, full of the sort of self-examination that humility inspires us all to undertake since we are all unaware of some issue or group or reality. That doesn't mean there's a rough equivalence between the anti-Black attitudes of white folk and the limitations of vision about sexuality, gender, and class that hamper Black life. But we should all scrutinize our own worldviews and purge them as much as possible of the poisonous prejudices that plague our existence.

Dear Sandra, these differences among us Black folk might account for the understandable confusion of white allies at this pivotal moment in history. Some Black folk demand that white folk speak up and be brave in the face of racial injustice. Many white folk want to get things right and hope to spare themselves unnecessary shame and embarrassment as they speak and act. Thus, they reach out to Black folk to ask how they can serve with the greatest care and impact — only to be met by some Black folk, tired and exhausted, who proclaim that they won't assist white folk in the fraught journey to racial reckoning. The best white allies are not easily dissuaded from the task at hand: their feelings are not easily hurt, their determination to help is not easily derailed, and their desire to make progress toward racial justice is not easily discouraged.

It should be plain by now that there are different levels of membership in the community of white allies. There is the introductory membership, through which white allies get woke and realize they've got a great deal of work to do and must read and reflect to become more familiar with the racial problems of our culture. Associate membership builds on white folk reading while they also attend gatherings of like-minded white folk in book clubs, civic groups, or church associations to further clarify their unique roles in the struggle for racial justice. Within the corporate world they make efforts to deepen diversity and broaden inclusion of Black and other voices in the reimagining of corporate goals and practices. Advanced membership pushes the envelope further and finds white folk in positions of power atop corporate and political structures leveraging their influence to bring far greater racial justice to the social and political realm. This includes a concerted effort to challenge white privilege, white fragility, and white comfort, and to argue for the overhaul of unjust social relationships in all communities of color and wherever else injustice prevails. Finally, lifetime membership is for white folk seeking to embody the principles of radical justice while dismantling oppressive systems and racist structures. The police have recently been in the crosshairs of such allies. Lifetime membership often puts white allies next to Black folk at social protests, and if necessary it puts their bodies in line to get arrested, to endure police brutality, and in some cases to make the ultimate sacrifice, like John Brown and James Reeb, Michael Schwerner and Andrew Goodman, and Viola Liuzzo and Heather Heyer.

Today, perhaps one of the most useful ways white allies can challenge white comfort is to admit that the embrace of Donald Trump and his troubling ideas is duplicitous: whites want to distrance themselves from the racist past while endorsing Trump's racist beliefs in the present day. For decades, many whites have spurned affirmative action in the belief that it rewards undeserving Black folk with jobs or diplomas when, in truth, mediocre white folk have cornered the market on social goods because of systemic racism.

Some of these same folks think they can protect their beliefs by taking refuge in the presidency of a man who brazenly embraces naked bigotry. Trump permits his followers to revel in their comfort without apology while dismissing as baseless scolds those who would dare to chastise them. It is Trump's shameless prejudice that emboldens his followers to follow suit. It falls to genuine white allies to take to task as best they can the unprincipled white nationalists who morally manipulate the white masses.

To fight white comfort it is critical to better understand systemic and structural racism, since racial hostility and anti-Black attitudes are best viewed as forces bigger than one's personal beliefs or sentiments. It's not that racism doesn't have personal effect; it is that its biggest impact ranges far beyond what any individual can say or do. There are many ways to get at how racism functions in our society. One of them is viewing racism and its offshoots in structural terms, as a tree. First, racism is the seed that is planted or that falls onto the ground. This analogy captures two dimensions of racism. On the one hand, it reflects the conscious intent to sow hate of Black folk and other people of color. On the other hand, the seed falls from the tree as a matter of course — organically — without intent to do harm, although its growth can nevertheless cause great damage. Seeds are dispersed by wind, or the trends of a culture; by water, or the sustaining body of racist belief that gives them life; and by the animals who eat or accidentally transport them, or the people who inherit and transmit hate.

If racism is the individual seed, then the ground onto which it falls is the system, the soil that creates the opportunity for the seed to grow into a tree. On the forest floor the dense propagation of race hate encourages the growth of more hate, as on the Internet and social media. There are open fields, or the vast reaches of untilled young minds that are fertile ground for racist belief. There are yards, too, or those well-manicured spaces in fraternities and sororities and other social groups where racist beliefs can thrive. From the seed grows the sprout, which is racism in its first blush of prejudice before it blossoms into mature hate. (Of course, not all seeds germinate — sometimes hatred misses an opportunity to take hold in a mind or family because an adult deliberately discourages its growth.)

The sprout seeks sunlight, or the bright affirmations of racism offered by Western philosophers in books that teach race hatred and the belief in Black inferiority as central to enlightenment reason. That sunlight, those thinkers, produce leaves, or other racist books whose literary leaves are imprinted with bigotry and stereotypes. The process permits the tree to make its own food through photosynthesis, in a self-sustaining process where those books and thinkers feed off their own carbon dioxide, or toxic reasoning, and drink in water to sustain the justification of Black inferiority.

The fledgling tree, the theory of Black inferiority, grows steadily and hardens into discrimination, the effort to target Black folk with unequal and disparaging treatment. As the upstart tree grows, as racism develops, it seeks out more light, or more rational justifications for itself, and its roots sink deeper into the soil, the system, into sermons, lectures, and campaign stump speeches.

Just as the seedling grows in competition, and later often in concert, with other seedlings, racism too takes root and sprouts in the midst of misogyny, sexism, patriarchy, homophobia, transphobia, classism, and the like. And it must fend off threats: the fire of, for instance, King's oratory and Fannie Lou Hamer's vivid speech; floods, the washing through of tides of resistance and protest; ice, the freezing effect of antiracist books and thinkers. At this stage the seedling is most vulnerable, but if racism can hold on despite movements aimed at wiping it out, it will thrive. Thus, it becomes a sapling — it becomes a junior member of an archconservative organization that spouts scientific racism, say, or it becomes connected to an older racist figure, much like Stephen Miller's white nationalist beliefs were nurtured by David Horowitz, an older white nationalist.

Eventually, a mature tree grows, and the full-fledged racist thinking and practice, of the sort produced by white supremacy, continues to be supported by the ground and system that nurtured it. Now, as the tree drops its own seeds, it nurtures more racist figures and feeds even more white supremacist thought and action. And it goes on and on and on and on — the white "again" reseeding itself and producing a forest of hate and a systemic racist groundswell.

Dear Sandra, if we are to have a true reckoning with race, we must challenge white comfort in all its valence and cadence, in all its voice and vision, in all its tone and shade. The quest for white comfort has killed Black people and other folk of color for far too long. And there is so much more to systemic racism; it resides in school systems that prevent kids from flourishing, and in healthcare systems that deny Black and other folk of color equal access to quality hospitals, medical treatment, and insurance. It throws up roadblocks to fair and just treatment in the criminal justice system. It creates havoc in our nation's housing system, where Black folk and other people of color are routinely denied the same loans and advantages offered to white folk. Employment prospects for Black folk are abysmal; an important study shows that white men with criminal records often have a better shot at a given job than Black men with no criminal records. And our system of government has used official means to prevent Black flourishing on every level for centuries, from voting to serving in the military to getting good jobs in the public sphere. The institutions of American life breed racial injustice and fuel racial inequality. Most every entity whose name ends in the word "system" has been used to methodically exclude Black bodies and to prevent Black well-being — while providing comfort to the white masses.

Dear, dear Sandra, as we reckon with the crisis unleashed by George Floyd's death, we must reckon with the white comfort that permitted white folk to ignore other deaths like his for centuries. Perhaps because of him, and Breonna Taylor, Ahmaud Arbery, Elijah McClain, Hadiya Pendleton, you, and too many others to name, we will finally come to grips with white comfort and finally proclaim three words that are the very heartbeat of our country and culture, slowly, deliberately, and with appropriate emphasis: Black. Lives. Matter.

Selling worse than flogging. My husband was sold six years ago. My heart has bled ever since, and is not well yet. I have been flogged many times, since he was torn from me but my back has healed in time.

— UNNAMED ENSLAVED WOMAN


If it were not for our hopes, our hearts would break; we poor slaves always cherish hopes of better times.

— WILLIAM GRIMES


So they lived through their tragic moment until at last they came out on the other side, saluting the fulfillment of their hopes and their faith.

— HOWARD THURMAN

# POSTLUDE:
# EVERGREEN HOPE

Dear Rev. Clementa Pinckney,

My brother clergyman, I can't tell you how many times I've thought of you since you were tragically gunned down in the church where you preached the Word. I thought of you when I preached at the Conference of National Black Churches interracial meeting in Charleston, South Carolina, six months after your death, and as I sat in the pew of your church to listen to Bishop John Bryant breathe fire on the strongholds of evil. I think of you sometimes as I try to speak for the God who called us both to preach. I marvel at your dignity, your courage, and your willingness to host strangers even at the risk of your life. I think of Martin Luther King Jr. too, America's greatest witness for the God we serve and the Word we preach. And I think of what it means to take the gospel seriously and to say we will die for it, something that you and Dr. King share.

You represent so much of what I hold precious: the ministry, politics, public service. I wish there were more folks like you who didn't think that God stayed out of politics, and that politics shouldn't have anything to do with God — although, given how some folk bring the two together, I'd just as soon leave God out of the entire insane affair we frequently make of that arena. Dr. King said he'd sometimes pass white churches and, thinking of their abysmal track record when it came to racial justice, he'd wonder, Who is their God? It is still a relevant question. How can folk say they love God and yet hate so many of God's children — Black folk, poor folk, gay and lesbian folk, trans folk, and a whole lot more? Either you love God and you hate injustice, or you hate the folk God loves and therefore you don't really know or love God. At least not the God I've come to know, not the Being I believe in, the uplifting energy and loving spirit that courses through this universe.

Although you've only been dead a few years now, it seems like another age when you lost your life just shy of your forty-second birthday. You were leading Bible study that June evening for fewer than a dozen members of the historic Emanuel African Methodist Episcopal Church, where you pastored, when a twenty-one-year-old white stranger named Dylann Roof joined the gathering. The Black church is so warm and welcoming that you made him feel right at home. Roof took supreme advantage of that opportunity and unloaded his .45 pistol on the lot of you, killing nine folk and injuring one other person. Roof confessed that he deliberately sought you out and committed this act of unconscionable bigotry to provoke a race war.

As a man of the cloth who began preaching at thirteen and pastoring a church at eighteen, I can only imagine that your faith was exceedingly strong. I hear your mother named you after one of my heroes, the great baseball player Roberto Clemente, who died in a plane crash as he was en route to deliver aid to earthquake victims in Nicaragua. You, too, died in an act of sacrifice for the greater good. As a preacher now for more than forty-one years, I have tried to make sense of the ceaseless killing of Black folk. In the midst of so much death, how can we still hope?

I know that many folks think Black hope should have gone out of style with bell-bottoms and platform heels — or even long before that. Some folk think hope is the killer itself. They think that the expectation that something might change, could change, is mass delusion and rank absurdity. It raises our blood pressure, gives us heart trouble, and floods our bodies with sugary poison. If we were to surrender such hope and replace it with, say, circumstantial defeatism and strategic hopelessness, we'd be able to accept that our only hope is to learn how to cope better.

I understand that view and don't disparage those who hold it. But something just won't let me wiggle free of my theological captivity to hope. To be certain, it's not a vain hope, nor one that is fanciful. Mine is rather a darker hope, one located in the guts of trauma and tragedy as I look on the suffering we have endured because of the pandemic of systemic racism and institutional oppression. I just can't give it up, this hope that seems evergreen and yet ever elusive, often seeming to disappear at the moments we need it most, a fugitive hope — a hope against hope, as the Bible phrases it, which means there is little warrant for its existence and scant justification for its persistence. And yet here I am and there it is. My hope doesn't rest on what good white folk might do, and the change we can force if we are faithful — well, at least not entirely. My hope doesn't stand on the premises of rational argument or eloquent speech, or sermons and essays, or letters and books, although I want to use those forms and more to shape my agony into useful witness. My hope, finally, rests in a force, a Being, whose outlines I can't discern with my eyes nor prove with my mind or mouth, and yet here I am and there She is. There He resides.

So, Rev. Pinckney, if you gave your life for it, the least I can do is spend my life in service of a love that never ends, a faith that sometimes crumbles, a hope that seems, somehow, forever to endure, in ways I can neither understand nor explain. My fellow Americans, I can't prove it, but I believe that this hope is bigger than all the hell and hate we must confront as we battle for a better world. I believe it is true with all my heart. I hope it will, as the old folk of my faith say, prop us up on every leaning side and spare us from dangers seen and unseen. I will keep fighting and reckoning with our past and present to make a better future. I hope you will too.

# ACKNOWLEDGMENTS

I'd like to thank my five families. First, my publishing family: my extraordinary and heroic editor, Elisabeth Dyssegaard, her loyal and attentive assistant, Alex Brown, my sublime and top-notch managing editor, Alan Bradshaw, my meticulous and conscientious copyeditor, Sue Warga, my wonderful publicist, Gabi Gantz, my tremendous marketing guru, Martin Quinn, visionary jacket designer David Baldeosingh Rotstein, gifted production manager Jeremy Haiting, talented text designer Meryl Levavi, the amazing associate publisher Laura Clark, the incomparable Jennifer Enderlin, my publisher (and fellow *Godfather* aficionado), and the true Don, the CEO of Macmillan, Don Weisberg (and fellow basketball junkie). And I can't forget the peerless SMP chairman, Sally Richardson. Second, my representative family: the brilliant Tanya McKinnon and Carol Taylor, agents, but so

235

much more, and first-rate intellectuals too. Third, my family of service and assistance: my scholarly teaching assistant, Marie Plaisime, who has really been my co-teacher; and my indispensable personal assistant, Ms. Carolyn Brown, though that title hardly begins to capture the incredible help she gives me on a daily basis. Fourth, my university family — at Georgetown, President John J. DeGioia, his chief of staff, Joseph Ferrara, and Provost Robert Groves; at Vanderbilt, Chancellor Daniel Diermeier, Provost Susan Wente, Dean John Geer, Dean Emilie Townes, and Department of African American & Diaspora Studies Chair Tracy Sharpley-Whiting — for your incredible support. Finally, thanks to my loving family: my amazing mother, Addie Mae Dyson, my brothers Gregory and Brian (RIP to our brothers Anthony and Everett), my nieces and nephew, grandnieces and grandnephews, and my children, Michael II, Maisha (and her daughter, Layla), and Mwata (and his sons Mosi and Max) — the triumphant trilogy of mighty M's, all presided over by the matchless and marvelous matriarch, Marcia! Love you all!

# SOURCES

## PRELUDE

On George Floyd's death, see Haley Willis et al., "New Footage Shows Delayed Medical Response to George Floyd," *New York Times,* August 11, 2020, https://www .nytimes.com/2020/08/11/us/george-floyd -body-cam-full-video.html.

## CHAPTER 1

For biographical details on Emmett Till, see "The Shocking Story of Approved Killing in Mississippi," *Look Magazine,* January 24, 1956, pp. 46–50, and Martin Luther King, "Who Speaks for the South?" in James M. Washington, *A Testament of Hope: The Essential Writings and Speeches of Martin Luther King, Jr.* (New York: Har-perCollins, 1986), p. 92.

For Martin Luther King Jr. on Till's death,

see "Address Delivered at a Meeting Launching the SCLC Crusade for Citizenship at Greater Bethel AME Church," on February 12, 1958, in Miami, Florida. Martin Luther King, Jr., Research and Education Institute, https://kinginstitute.stanford.edu/king-papers/documents/address-delivered-meeting-launching-sclc-crusade-citizenship-greater-bethel.

For Central Park dog incident, see Stephanie Guerilus, "Woman Falsely Claims Black Man Threatened Life in Central Park," The Grio, https://thegrio.com/2020/05/25/white-woman-black-man-central-park/, and Brian Price, Checkey Beckford, and Kiki Intarasuwan, "Woman in Racial Central Park Confrontation Is Fired from Job, Gives Up Dog," NBC 4 New York, https://www.nbcnewyork.com/news/local/central-park-confrontation-goes-viral-white-woman-calls-cop-on-black-birder/2431773/.

For generational racist views, see Scott Clement, "Millennials Are Just as Racist as Their Parents," Washington Post, June 23, 2015, https://www.washingtonpost.com/news/wonk/wp/2015/06/23/millennials-are-just-as-racist-as-their-parents/.

**CHAPTER 2**

On Walter E. Brown, Cornelius Brown, Theodoric Johnson, and Leroy Perry, see Manning Marable, *How Capitalism Underdeveloped Black America* (Boston: South End Press, 1999), pp. 213–214.

On George Floyd: Ny Magee, "George Floyd's 2nd Grade Essay Reveals He Wanted to Be a Supreme Court Justice," The Grio, June 5, 2020, https://thegrio.com/2020/06/05/george-floyd-2nd-grade-letter-supreme-court-justice/. See also Callan Gray, "Court Filings Shed More Light on Former Officer Thomas Lane's Training," ABC 5 Eyewitness News, https://kstp.com/news/court-filings-shed-more-light-on-former-minneapolis-police-officer-thomas-lane-training/5787727/ and " 'We Have to Do This Right': Hennepin County Attorney Mike Freeman Says George Floyd Investigation Will Take Time," WCCO 4 CBS Minnesota, May 28, 2020, https://minnesota.cbslocal.com/2020/05/28/we-have-to-do-this-right-henncpin-county-attorney-mike-freeman-says-george-floyd-investigation-will-take-time/. For transcripts of interactions between George Floyd and the cops, see staff reports, "Read the Transcript of

Thomas Lane's Body Camera Footage During George Floyd Call," and "Read the Transcript of J. Alexander Kueng's Body Camera Footage During George Floyd Call," *Minnesota Star Tribune,* July 9 and July 16, 2020.

For the names of the lost, see SCAPE Black Lives Matter list at https://www.scapestudio.com/news/2020/06/black-lives-matter/.

## CHAPTER 3

The section on slavery in this chapter was informed by the following superb books: Alan Taylor, *The Internal Enemy: Slavery and War in Virginia, 1772–1832* (New York: W.W. Norton, 2013); Sylviane A. Diouf, *Slavery's Exiles: The Story of the American Maroons* (New York: New York University Press, 2014); Eric Foner, *Gateway to Freedom: The Hidden History of the Underground Railroad* (New York: W.W. Norton, 2015); Steven Hahn, *A Nation Without Borders: The United States and Its World in an Age of Civil Wars, 1830–1910* (New York: Viking, 2016); and Sally E. Hadden, *Slave Patrols: Law and Violence in Virginia and the Carolinas* (Cambridge, MA: Harvard University Press, 2001).

On the 1619 Project, see *New York Times,* https://www.nytimes.com/interactive/2019/ 08/14/magazine/1619-america-slavery .html; on criticism of it, see Adam Serwer, "The Fight over the 1619 Project Is Not About the Facts," *Atlantic,* December 23, 2019, https://www.theatlantic.com/ideas/ archive/2019/12/historians-clash-1619 -project/604093/, and Bryan Armen Graham, "Tom Cotton Calls Slavery 'Necessary Evil' in Attack on New York Times' 1619 Project," *Guardian,* July 26, 2020, https://www.theguardian.com/world/ 2020/jul/26/tom-cotton-slavery-necessary -evil-1619-project-new-york-times.

## CHAPTER 4

On Kobe Bryant: Ben McGrath, "The Fourth Quarter," *New Yorker,* March 24, 2014.

## CHAPTER 5

On Fannie Lou Hamer: "It's In Your Hands," 1971, History Is a Weapon, http:// hiaw.org/defcon1/yourhandshamer.html. For the study on white men with criminal records getting offered better jobs than Black men with no records, see Devah

Pager, *Marked: Race, Crime, and Finding Work in an Era of Mass Incarceration* (Chicago: University of Chicago Press, 2007).

# ABOUT THE AUTHOR

**Michael Eric Dyson** is one of America's premier public intellectuals and the author of more than twenty books, including the *New York Times* bestsellers *JAY-Z, Tears We Cannot Stop,* and *What Truth Sounds Like.* He is a contributing opinion writer for the *New York Times* and a contributing editor of *ESPN's The Undefeated.* Dyson is winner of two NAACP Image awards and the recipient of the 2020 Langston Hughes Festival Medallion. Former President Barack Obama has noted: "Everybody who speaks after Michael Eric Dyson pales in comparison."

The employees of Thorndike Press hope you have enjoyed this Large Print book. All our Thorndike, Wheeler, and Kennebec Large Print titles are designed for easy reading, and all our books are made to last. Other Thorndike Press Large Print books are available at your library, through selected bookstores, or directly from us.

For information about titles, please call:
(800) 223-1244

or visit our website at:
gale.com/thorndike

To share your comments, please write:
Publisher
Thorndike Press
10 Water St., Suite 310
Waterville, ME 04901